D0198530

CULTURE SMART!
AFGHANISTAN

Moska Najib and Nazes Afroz

·K·U·P·E·R·A·R·D·

Mar 2014

ISBN 978 1 85733 679 5
This book is also available as an e-book: eISBN 978 1 85733 680 1

British Library Cataloguing in Publication Data
A CIP catalogue entry for this book is available from the
British Library

First published in Great Britain
by Kuperard, an imprint of Bravo Ltd
59 Hutton Grove, London N12 8DS
Tel: +44 (0) 20 8446 2440 Fax: +44 (0) 20 8446 2441
www.culturesmart.co.uk
Inquiries: sales@kuperard.co.uk

Distributed in the United States and Canada
by Random House Distribution Services
1745 Broadway, New York, NY 10019
Tel: +1 (212) 572-2844 Fax: +1 (212) 572-4961
Inquiries: csorders@randomhouse.com

Series Editor Geoffrey Chesler
Design Bobby Birchall

Printed in Malaysia

About the Authors

MOSKA NAJIB is a journalist. Born in Afghanistan, she was educated in India and Switzerland, where she graduated with distinction in International Communications. She has worked with the BBC Bureau in Delhi, where she was a producer and reporter, covering news and social issues all over India for BBC TV and World Service radio. Her photo-features have appeared on the BBC News Web site. Moska has lived most of her life outside Afghanistan, but is deeply rooted in Afghan history, culture, and traditions.

NAZES AFROZ was a newspaper journalist in Calcutta before moving to London to work for the BBC World Service, most recently as a senior executive. He has traveled extensively in India, reporting on politics, social conflicts, the environment, and human rights, and in South and Central Asia, the Middle East, and Africa. Nazes has been visiting Afghanistan regularly for the last ten years for the BBC. He is also a photographer; his work appears in various publications and on BBC Web sites.

The authors are currently working together on photography and research projects involving Afghanistan and India.

The Culture Smart! series is continuing to expand.
For further information and latest titles visit
www.culturesmart.co.uk

The publishers would like to thank **CultureSmart!**Consulting for its help in researching and developing the concept for this series.

CultureSmart!Consulting creates tailor-made seminars and consultancy programs to meet a wide range of corporate, public-sector, and individual needs. Whether delivering courses on multicultural team building in the USA, preparing Chinese engineers for a posting in Europe, training call-center staff in India, or raising the awareness of police forces to the needs of diverse ethnic communities, it provides essential, practical, and powerful skills worldwide to an increasingly international workforce.

For details, visit www.culturesmartconsulting.com

CultureSmart!Consulting and **CultureSmart!** guides have both contributed to and featured regularly in the weekly travel program "Fast Track" on BBC World TV.

contents

Map of Afghanistan

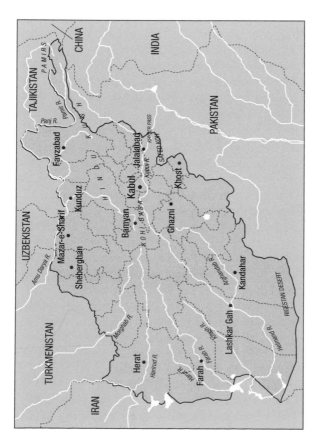

introduction

When describing the inexplicable attraction of this country, travelers often talk about the "Afghanistan bug" that bites first-time visitors and makes them fall madly in love with it. For most people around the world, however, the very mention of Afghanistan evokes an image of a remote, wretched place embroiled in continuous war and conflict.

Afghanistan has been in the headlines for all the wrong reasons for three decades, despite being a land of breathtaking beauty, with a rich history and a fascinating tapestry of ethnicities and cultures. Sitting at the crossroads of several civilizations, for centuries, unwillingly and often unknowingly, it has been drawn into the geopolitical intrigues and rivalries of international power play. This has often led to Afghans fighting each other; and foreign military or political interventions have contributed to the ongoing conflict that has displaced millions from their homes and land in recent times.

In the midst of these upheavals live a people who are among the most hospitable and honorable in the world. They have always led a contented and simple life with only the most basic amenities. The country's rough, rugged landscape has charmed travelers over the centuries, with the imposing snow-capped mountains of the Hindu Kush, the Pamirs dotted with idyllic green valleys, or the vast expanses of the semi-desert arid regions.

These early travelers were also fascinated by the age-old traditions and customs that still exist as if in a time warp. Afghan society is organized mainly along ethnic and tribal lines, but ethnic identity becomes irrelevant in the face of a common threat. There are also many shared values and unwritten codes of conduct that govern personal relations, which are not taken lightly. Outsiders have always been confounded by the two extreme experiences of the ferocity of the Afghan people and by their boundless generosity and hospitality. Although they are inherently suspicious of foreigners, they will protect those same foreigners with their lives if they decide to give them refuge.

Today the Afghans are straddling the conflicting realities of the modern world and their ancient traditions, for which they are ready to sacrifice their lives. Their values are being reshaped slowly by their interactions with the outside world and by the presence of the massive number of foreigners engaged in the nation-building project since the overthrow of the Taliban regime in 2001.

In *Culture Smart! Afghanistan* we have set out to explain the country's history, its people—their habits, customs, traditions, idiosyncrasies, suspicions about foreigners, and patterns of behavior—and its current place in the world. The book will give you an idea of how to interact with the Afghans, how to interpret their behavior, and how to behave appropriately in their company, whether in personal or business exchanges. It will prepare you for a journey through a society that is difficult to navigate and often hard to understand. Stay the course, and the rewards will be great.

Key Facts

Official Name	Islamic Republic of Afghanistan	Afghanistan became an Islamic Republic in 1992, after the collapse of the Communist regime.
Capital City	Kabul	Population approx. 3.5 million
Main Cities	The second-largest city is Kandahar, which is primarily Pashto-speaking. Other major cities: Mazar-e-Sharif, Herat, Bamiyan, Jalalabad, Ghazni, Badakshan.	History shows that whoever secures Kandahar controls the rest of the country. There are 34 provinces in Afghanistan.
Population	30,419,928 (July 2012). Population growth is 2.22%.	More than 5.7 million refugees have returned since 2002.
Ethnic Makeup	Approx. 42% are Pashtun, 27% Tajik, 9% Hazara, 9% Uzbek; others are Turkmen, Baluch, and other minorities.	
Area	251,773 sq. miles (652,225 sq. km)	Mount Noshaq, the highest mountain at 24,580 ft (7,492 m), is in the northeast.
Climate	As varied as its geographical landscape. The weather is very cold in winter and very hot in summer.	Four seasons: spring, March to May; summer, June to August; fall, September to November; winter, November to March
Languages	Dari (50%) and Pashto (35%) are the two official languages. 11% speak Turkic languages, primarily Uzbek and Turkmen.	

Religion	The state religion is Islam.	Sunni Muslims make up about 80% of the population, Shia Muslims about 19% and other religions 1%.
Government	Islamic Republic. Two houses of parliament: the Meshrano Jirga (Upper House) and the Wolesi Jirga (Lower House).	The president, elected for a five-year term, is head of state. He is also the commander-in-chief of the armed forces.
Business Hours	Government offices and banks are open from 9:00 a.m. to 4:00 p.m.	Official weekend is Friday (only).
Currency	Afghani (Afg). US $1= AFN 51 (2012)	US dollars are widely accepted. It's better to carry cash with you.
Media	Media outlets, incl. private TV stations, have mushroomed. State broadcaster is Radio Television Afghanistan (RTA).	Tolo TV is the most popular national station. Media laws ban material that is deemed to be against Islamic law.
Electricity	220 volts, 50 Hz	2-pronged plugs. Outages frequent
Video/TV	PAL system	
Internet Domain	.af	
Telephone	Afghanistan's country code is 93. To call abroad, dial 00.	Limited fixed-line service. Increasing use of cell phones.
Time Zone	GMT + 4.5 hours. There is no daylight saving.	Clocks are an hour ahead of Iran and 30 minutes behind the other neighbors.

LAND & PEOPLE

BORDERS AND BOUNDARIES

Afghanistan's geography has for centuries been its curse. Strategically located at the crossroads of major trade routes, the country has long been fought over as the seat of expanding empires. Its rugged and forbidding terrain is sandwiched between three major regions: the Indian Subcontinent to the southeast, Central Asia to the north, and the Iranian plateau to the west.

Almost as large as the state of Texas, this landlocked nation shares boundaries with six neighboring countries. Its longest border is with Pakistan, accounting for the entire southern and eastern frontier. Approximately 1,640 miles (2,640 km) long, the border is named after Sir Mortimer Durand, the British diplomat who arbitrarily drew a pencil line along a map in 1893, dividing British Indian territory from a fiercely independent Afghanistan.

To the west is Iran, a neighbor with an overlapping history and deep ties of language, ethnicity, and culture. The provinces of Herat, Farah, and Nimruz, bordering Iran, are a favorite transit corridor for drug traffickers, who smuggle their cargoes to dealers in Europe and beyond.

In the north are the Republics of Tajikistan, Uzbekistan, and Turkmenistan. When the Soviet Union collapsed in the 1990s, Afghanistan found that the number of its northern neighbors had tripled. Sharing the shortest border in the extreme northeast is China. Only 47 miles (76 km) long, it is located in the remote and largely inaccessible Pamir Mountain range that was once part of the ancient Silk Road trade route.

Without a doubt, Afghanistan's history and politics have largely been determined by its extraordinary geographic location. Migrating groups have passed through this country and left behind a blend of ethnic, linguistic, and cultural influences. Afghanistan's borders and boundaries on the Silk Road, the great caravan route that once linked the markets of Asia to those of the Western world, have today become flashpoints in the geopolitics of the region.

LANDSCAPE

A land of great variety and contrast, two-thirds of
Afghanistan is mountainous terrain with barely any
vegetation, and half of the remaining part is desert.
The towering peaks of the Hindu Kush separate the
northern provinces from the rest of the country.
Running northeast to southwest through the entire
length of central Afghanistan, this rugged mountain
range divides the country into three distinct
geographic zones: the central highlands, the
northern plains, and the southern plateau.

Forming part of the Himalayas, the central
highlands include the main Hindu Kush range.
This is a region of deep, narrow valleys and lofty
mountains with numerous peaks over 20,000 feet
(6,096 m) high. In the extreme eastern part of the
country, the highest peaks of the Hindu Kush tower
at almost 24,000 feet (7,315 m) above sea level. The
mountains descend in altitude as they stretch
westward to Iran. The areas in and around the
Hindu Kush are prone to earthquakes, in particular
in the northeastern province of Badakhshan.

Midway in the Hindu Kush, in the central part of the country, is the Koh-e-Baba range that feeds Afghanistan's three most important rivers—the Kabul, which flows east to join the Indus River in Attok, in Pakistan; the Helmand-Arghandab, which waters the Kandahar, Lashkar Gah, and Sistan areas of the south before disappearing into the marshy lakes of the Hamun-i-Helmand, mainly in Iran; and the Hari Rud, or Herat, River, which flows west past the city of Herat and meanders north to Turkmenistan, where it disappears in the Kara-Kum Desert. Most of the water in Afghanistan comes from these river systems, which carry the snowmelt from the mountains into the lower areas of the country.

The fertile land of Afghanistan lies in the northern plains, which extend from the Iranian border to the foothills of the Pamirs near Tajikistan. Nomads graze sheep and goats on the grasslands of this region, which is also rich in mineral deposits and natural gas. Its fertile foothills slope gently toward the Amu Darya, or Oxus, River. The northern plains region is heavily populated, and the abundance of the agricultural land makes it the breadbasket of the country.

Sandy deserts and semi-desert plains are a key feature of the south, with the Rigestan Desert making up about a quarter of the area. The high, arid plateau extends into Iran and Pakistan. To the west of Rigestan lies the Dasht-e-Margoh ("Desert of Death"), covered with salt flats. Summer dust storms and sandstorms are common in the deserts, particularly in the southwestern parts of this region.

Afghanistan has several famous lakes. Hidden in the Koh-e-Baba range, at an altitude of 9,514 feet (2,900 m), is the Band-e-Amir—a series of six stunning lakes separated by natural dams of travertine. Nothing prepares one for the sudden blaze of sapphire blue and turquoise waters, which are often as smooth as glass, perfectly reflecting the mountains that surround them.

CLIMATE
The climate in Afghanistan is as varied as its landscape. While the mountains of the northeast have dry, cold winters, the areas bordering Pakistan are influenced by the Indian monsoons that usually arrive between July and September, bringing rains and humidity.

There are four distinct seasons. The winter days, from December through February, are generally sunny and crisp, with several heavy snowfalls in the mountains. Barring the extreme southern parts of Afghanistan, temperatures plummet below zero as soon as the sun sets—so thick, warm clothing is a must during this time of year. Spring, on the other hand, is one of the most pleasant times to explore the country. From April to May the dusty mountains and arid deserts burst into life,

studded with blooms of wild flowers and fruit blossoms. Afghanistan is then at its loveliest; but the spring melt can bring trouble of its own, with heavy rains and floods making many roads impassable or extremely difficult to use.

Summers are cool and comfortable in the mountains throughout the months of June, July, and August, but it gets very hot and dusty in the north and south of the country. Cities like Kandahar, Mazar-e-Sharif, and Jalalabad swelter in the heat, with the temperature rising to 104°F (40°C).

However, the ideal season to travel and visit Afghanistan is fall. A riot of colors brightens the days from September through November. This is harvest time, and it brings the best of Afghan fruits—sweet melons, fresh grapes, and ruby-red pomegranates known to be the best in the world.

THE LAND OF THE AFGHANS

Afghanistan has never been inhabited by one single ethnic group. Its people form a diverse and complex mosaic of ethnicities—a reflection of its geographic location and its historical significance as the crossroads of Asia, where conquerors and occupiers settled or passed through.

According to the latest census, Afghanistan's population of thirty million people is divided into seven major ethnic groups—Pashtuns, Tajiks, Hazaras, Uzbeks, Aimaqs, Turkmen, and Baluch—and many smaller ones.

Society is organized mainly along ethnic and tribal lines. Most Afghans can recognize what part of the country someone hails from based on his tribe, and identify more with those who share their local language and culture. However, while their loyalty is to their tribe, being identified as an "Afghan" takes precedence. This patchwork of ethnic identities becomes irrelevant when Afghans feel threatened by a common enemy who seeks to control their country—the land of the Afghans.

ETHNIC BREAKDOWN	
Pashtun	42%
Tajik	27%
Hazara	9%
Uzbek	9%
Aimaqs	4%
Turkmen	3%
Baluchi	2%
Others	4%
(Source: The World Factbook, CIA, 2012)	

Pashtuns

Pashtuns (also known as Pakhtuns or Pathans)—Caucasians with tall figures and distinctive dark eyes—form the largest ethnic group in Afghanistan, constituting about two-fifths of the country's population. The oldest continuous inhabitants of the region, they are Sunni Muslims who were traditionally farmers and semi-

nomads, their homeland extending along the eastern and southern borders of the country. Claiming a common ancestor, language (Pashto), and religion, the Pashtuns are egalitarian, and rule themselves within their separate clans (*quam*) and subclans (*khel*) through councils composed of the leading men of each family. The two dominant tribal groups are the Ghilzai and the Durrani. The Ghilzai live predominantly in the eastern mountainous region of the country and are regarded as a conservative tribe. The Durrani are the educated and more liberal clan, living mainly in the southern areas.

Since the mid-eighteenth century, the Pashtuns have dominated the country's politics. Known as strong and hardy fighters ("the men of the sword"), they are an honor-bound people who will fight to maintain or recover their pride under *Pashtunwali*, the traditional code of ethics that has governed tribal affairs for thousands of years (see page 51).

> "Pukhtun with love will accompany you to hell, but with force not even to heaven."
> Khan Abdul Ghaffar Khan, the "Frontier Gandhi."

Tajiks

The second-largest ethnic group, the Tajiks live in the northeastern corner of the country, bordering Tajikistan. Believed to be of Iranian origin, they are tall, slender, fair-skinned Caucasians with blue or green eyes. They share the looks of the Iranian peoples, as well as their Persian language.

The Tajik community is not as tribal as the Pashtuns. When asked what people they are, most Tajiks will identify themselves with the particular valley, town, or region where they live. The term "Tajik" is mainly associated with those who do not belong to a tribal society, who speak Dari, and who are mostly Sunni Muslims.

Comprising more than a quarter of the country's population, the Tajiks of Afghanistan form the largest Tajik population outside their homeland in Tajikistan. Large numbers of Tajiks can be found in the cities of Herat, Kabul, Mazar-e-Sharif, and Ghazni. They are mainly agricultural, except in those towns and cities where many are artisans who engage in commercial activities. Conscious of their cultural tradition, the Tajiks have often been referred to as "the men of the pen."

Hazaras

In an isolated region in the country's central ranges, known as Hazarajat, is the second Dari-speaking group, the Hazaras. They form Afghanistan's largest Shiite minority, who have long been branded outsiders within the dominant Sunni Muslim population. Believed to be descendants of Genghis Khan's soldiers, their Mongoloid features—flat noses, broad cheeks, and narrow eyes—set them apart from other Afghans.

Traditionally on the bottom rung of Afghan society, Hazaras were exploited and considered a servant class. They have been discriminated against on religious grounds throughout the history of modern Afghanistan. Today, however, Hazaras run some of the country's leading press and media organizations.

Uzbeks

Afghanistan's fourth-largest ethnic group, the Uzbeks are descendants of the Turkic invaders of the

fifteenth century. They live in the agricultural regions north of the Hindu Kush, across the border from Uzbekistan. They speak their own Turkic dialect, Uzbeki, and identify themselves as Sunni Muslims.

While many practice agriculture, those living in towns are known as skillful artisans. Uzbeks have influenced Afghan culture, particularly in sport. They are thought to have introduced the national sport of Afghanistan, *buzkashi* (see Chapter 6).

Uzbeks have some different eating habits. Pasta, unusual in most Afghan dishes, is common in Uzbek cuisine, as are *mantoo*, which are steamed dumplings filled with onion and minced beef, and the noodle soup called *aush*. Uzbeki dress also differs, in that the men wear a long, striped *chapan* (a loose, cotton coat worn over a shirt and trousers), a small turban, and soft leather boots that fit tightly over woolen stockings and reach to the knees.

Others
A number of other ethnic groups live in small pockets within Afghanistan. The Aimaqs are a mixed

tribe composed of various ethnic groups, including Hazara, Baluch, and Tajik. Mainly farmers and herders, they live in the western areas of the provinces of Ghor, Badghis, and Herat. They are Sunni Muslims, and speak a dialect similar to Dari, mixed with Mongolian and Turkic words.

Although the Turkmen are one of Central Asia's major groups, they are a minority in Afghanistan. Mostly herders and craftspeople, they live across the border from Turkmenistan. In the aftermath of the Bolshevik Revolution, a large number fled to Afghanistan and settled in the area. The Turkmen have contributed greatly to the economy as breeders of Karakul sheep and weavers of Turkmen carpets.

The Kirghiz are in the Pamir Mountains, in the northeastern arm of Afghanistan. Most are herders who live in *yurts* (tents) that are easily moved from place to place. They measure their wealth in sheep, goats, and yaks.

In the southern deserts of Afghanistan, along the border with Pakistan and Iran, are the Baluchis. Mainly desert dwellers and herders, they are Sunnis.

As one of the groups with the longest ties to the region, the Nuristanis have lived in the eastern mountains ever since Alexander the Great traveled through Afghanistan. A linguistically distinct people, they speak several languages and dialects of Indo-Iranian origin. Under the reign of Amir Abdur Rahman, they were forcibly converted to Islam in the late nineteenth century. The Nuristanis have physical features similar to Europeans: they have fair skin, blond hair, and blue or green eyes, giving rise to the myth that they were the descendants of the Greeks from Alexander's time.

Other smaller groups consist of the Brahuis, Hindus, Sikhs, and Gujars, who originate from the Indian Subcontinent. The indigenous Jewish community is totally depleted in Afghanistan; currently, only one man remains to care for the synagogue in Kabul and keep the country's Jewish history alive.

A BRIEF HISTORY

Historians have called Afghanistan the "roundabout of the ancient world," and its history cannot be viewed in isolation. Over the centuries, it has been part of a series of empires, and subject to successions of migrations and invasions, at times making it a bloody testing ground.

Early History

While there has been some archaeological research carried out over the years, very little has covered Afghanistan's prehistory. Artifacts indicate that small farmers and herders inhabited the region some ten thousand years ago.

From very early times the region seems to have been connected by trade and commercial links stretching both east and west. Around 1500 BCE, tribes known as the Aryans, speaking an Indo-European language, began migrating into the northern plains.

The Achaemenid Empire (c. 550–33 BCE)

It was not until the sixth century BCE, however, that the region first appeared in recorded history, at the time of the Persian Achaemenid Empire.

Cyrus the Great of Persia extended the boundaries of the Achaemenid Empire into the region. Under his son-in-law, Darius I, the empire reached its greatest extent. Darius was a good statesman and an able administrator who organized the empire into satrapies, or provinces, and instituted a form of taxes to be collected by the satrap, or governor, of each province. The area of present-day Afghanistan formed several Achaemenid satrapies, among them Aria or Ariana (Herat), Bactria (Balkh), Arachosia (Ghazni and Kandahar), and Gandhara (the Kabul valley). Bactria, which later became known as Balkh, was reputedly the home of Zoroaster, who founded the religion that bears his name. The Persians embraced Zoroastrianism, and were instrumental in spreading it as far eastward as China.

Alexander of Macedon

Though the Achaemenid Empire was the largest the world had seen, in the fourth century BCE it began to disintegrate and gave way to the Greeks. Alexander III of Macedonia, known as "the Great," destroyed Persian power and overthrew the last Achaemenid emperor, Darius III, in 330 BCE.

After conquering the remaining Persian provinces, Alexander invaded Afghanistan. He launched two years of hard campaigning, pressing as far north as the Amu Darya (Oxus) River, but his army faced serious resistance in the Afghan tribal belt. The young conqueror, still in his twenties, realized that Afghanistan was a land "easy to march into, hard to march out of."

In a letter to his mother, Alexander wrote about his encounters with the Afghan tribesmen:

I am involved in the land of a "leonine" and brave people, where every foot of the ground is like a wall of steel confronting my soldiers. You have brought only one son into the world, but everyone in this land can be called an Alexander.

It was time for Alexander to move on, and he turned to the conquest of India. He sent the main part of his army through the Khyber Pass, while he himself led a small mobile force farther north up

the Kunar Valley to deal with the tribes in the mountains above the Kunar River, in the area known today as Nuristan. From here he turned eastward into Swat and continued campaigning in Punjab and Sind. But ultimately his fatigued troops had had enough of the unknown, and when their general proposed going farther east, beyond the Beas River in northwest India, they compelled him to retreat and forced a return to their homeland.

In spite of Alexander's short reign—he died of fever in Babylon in 323 BCE—he had a major impact on the history of Afghanistan, where he created cities, established a new political structure, and left a long-lasting Greek cultural and political presence in the region.

The Greco-Bactrian and Mauryan Empires
Three years after Alexander's death his vast empire was carved up by his generals. Afghanistan, geographically separated by the Hindu Kush, fell to Seleucus I Nicator, inheritor of Alexander's eastern conquests. At its height, the Selucid Empire that he

founded extended from Anatolia to India, and included the lands to the north of the Hindu Kush.

However, Chandragupta Maurya, founder of the Mauryan dynasty of India, wrested control of southern Afghanistan from Seleucus. In c. 305 BCE the Greeks and the Indians signed a peace treaty that formalized the status quo, with gifts of elephants and dynastic marriages. Under the Mauryan Emperor Ashoka the Great (269–231 BCE), Buddhism began to thrive in India and Afghanistan. The Edicts of Ashoka, carved on rocks and pillars in both countries, bear witness to the spread of Buddhism in the region.

While for the people living south of the Hindu Kush this was a period of peace and prosperity, Bactria in the north faced a turbulent time. In 250 BCE, a local governor, Diodotus I Soter, seceded from the Seleucid Empire and founded an independent Graeco-Bactrian kingdom. His successors expanded Bactrian rule, eventually spreading below the mountain range to cities where Mauryan power had been steadily declining since the death of their emperor.

Personal rivalries and military factions weakened the Bactrian dynasty. Though they were under pressure from migrating Parthians, it would be the Kushans (a nomadic subgroup of the Indo-European people known in China as the Yuezhi) who would enter ancient Afghanistan and establish an empire lasting almost four centuries.

The Kushan and Sassanid Dynasties

The name Kushan derives from the Chinese term *Guishang*. These Indo-European tribes from northwestern China reached Bactria around 135 BCE, where they adopted elements of its Hellenistic culture. They invaded the northern parts of Pakistan and India in the first century CE, and the empire they founded reached its greatest cultural and geographic extent under their most powerful ruler, the Buddhist emperor Kanishka (c. 127–151). The heart of his empire was centered on two capitals: the summer capital of Kapiska (north of Kabul) and the winter capital of Peshawar (in Pakistan today).

Situated exactly midway on the Silk Road caravan route, the Kushans exploited their position to gain vast wealth and, with it, great power. Their rise to world prominence brought immense changes to the lives of these former nomads. Having no traditions on which to build, they adapted to what they found in ways best suited to their way of life. What emerged was a vibrant indigenous culture born of the fusion of Graeco-Bactrian, Iranian, Indian, and Central Asian influences. Their emperors represented a variety of faiths, including Zoroastrianism, Buddhism, and possibly Saivism (a sect of Hinduism).

The revival of Buddhism and the emergence of Gandhara art are legacies of the Kushan era. Along

the ancient trade routes, stone monuments of Buddhist culture bear witness to the influence of this civilization on the arts in Afghanistan.

Civil wars followed Kanishka's death and weakened the Kushans, who ultimately fell under the sway of the Persian Sassanid Empire, successor state to the Parthians, in the third century CE. Although strong supporters of Zoroastrianism, the Sassanids tolerated Buddhism and allowed the construction of more Buddhist monasteries.

During their time, the monumental rock carvings

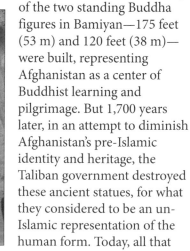

of the two standing Buddha figures in Bamiyan—175 feet (53 m) and 120 feet (38 m)— were built, representing Afghanistan as a center of Buddhist learning and pilgrimage. But 1,700 years later, in an attempt to diminish Afghanistan's pre-Islamic identity and heritage, the Taliban government destroyed these ancient statues, for what they considered to be an un-Islamic representation of the human form. Today, all that remains where they once stood are the mounds that were their feet.

The Advent of Islam, and the Ghaznavid and Ghurid Empires

In the seventh century CE, the Sassanids of Persia were defeated by a new, dynamic power that had swept out of the Arabian Desert. Marching under the banner of Islam, the Arab Muslims made their way into Afghanistan, captured Herat in 624, and brought the message of Islam to the south. In the north, however, they met with the same stiff resistance that Alexander had encountered centuries before. Despite a prolonged struggle, the Islamic advance became slow and difficult—every mile was heavily disputed and every conquered city rested only to revolt again.

Only in the tenth century would the Ghaznavid dynasty complete what the Arab Muslims had begun. Alptigin, a Turkish slave–soldier of the Persian Samanids of Bukhara, set out to found a kingdom of his own by capturing the fortress of Ghazni in 963. Though he died soon after this, his successors consolidated their power and went on to conquer Kabul, Bost, Balkh, and Herat, as well as part of western Persia. The fortress town of Ghazni, until then an insignificant place, became one of the political and cultural nerve centers of the Islamic world.

The sultans of Ghazni lived in splendor and fostered a renaissance of Persian culture. They built palaces and gardens in every major city of the realm. Sultan Mahmoud the Great (997–1030) was a patron of the arts, and in his courts gathered the most famous poets, artists, musicians, and craftsmen of the day. The Ghaznavid dynasty spread Islam to the Indian Subcontinent, but was unable to hold on to power for long, losing its western territories to the Seljuk Turks in 1040. A century later, the Ghurids delivered a deathblow.

The rulers of the remote kingdom of Ghur, high in the mountains east of Herat, rebelled against the Ghaznavid Empire, and captured and burned

Ghazni in 1148. Though their empire was short-lived, the Ghurids strengthened the presence of Islam in India as far as Delhi. They are best remembered as patrons of Persian architecture, leaving behind their greatest testament, the elegant Minaret of Jam, in Ghor province, built during the 1190s.

Genghis Khan and Timur the Lame

In the early thirteenth century the region was overrun by the mighty Mongol warlord Genghis Khan. A political and military mastermind, he had united the Mongol and other nomadic Central Asian tribes into a disciplined fighting force that went on to create an empire stretching from China to the Caspian Sea.

The Mongol invasion of Afghanistan in 1219 was a dark period. There was massive slaughter, cities were looted, and lands laid waste. The ruins of Shahr-i-Gholghola (the Cursed City) in Bamiyan is a reminder of the days of horror in 1221, when Genghis Khan destroyed the city and massacred its inhabitants as punishment for resistance.

Following Genghis Khan's death in 1227, his sons and their successors struggled for supremacy until late in the fourteenth century. Timur, the Turko-Mongol ruler of Samarkand (in present-day Uzbekistan) and an indirect descendant of Genghis Khan, conquered Afghanistan and incorporated it into his own vast empire.

Timur "the Lame," or Tamerlane, had a reputation for savage cruelty. He was also intellectually able, and a patron of the arts and sciences. But it was under the rule of his successor and son, Shah Rukh, that the Timurid Empire enjoyed its greatest glory. In Herat, the new capital, Shah Rukh began a cultural renaissance, building most of Afghanistan's major mosques and theological colleges. This fusion of Persian and Central Asian influences would leave a rich heritage for Afghanistan.

The Mughals, and the Birth of a Nation

Far to the north, in eastern Uzbekistan, lay the small kingdom of Fergana, where the young crown prince, Zahir-ud-din-Muhammad Babur, was a direct descendant of both Genghis Khan and Tamerlane. He was driven out of his father's dominion by Uzbek rebels led by his archrival Muhammad Shaybani, who took Samarkand, though only briefly. Babur crossed the Amu Darya (Oxus) River in 1504 and captured Kabul, then under the rule of a Kandahari warlord, thereby gaining a wealthy new kingdom. He would often, in his memoirs, the *Baburnama*, describe the beauty of his new home.

With expansion to the north and west blocked, Babur was drawn by the lure of India. In 1525, he left the rugged mountains of Afghanistan for the fertile north Indian plain. His defeat of the Delhi Sultanate in 1526 marked the beginning of the Mughal Empire in India. Though he ruled from his new capital in Agra, he never abandoned Kabul in his heart. In his memoirs he wrote despondently of his times in the new kingdom:

Hindustan is a country of few charms. There are no good-looking people, there is no social intercourse, no receiving or paying of visits, no genius or manners. In its handicrafts there is no form or symmetry, method, or quality. There are no good horses, no good dogs, no grapes, musk-melons, or first-rate fruits, no ice or cold water, no good bread or food cooked in the bazaars, no hot baths, no colleges, no candles, torches, or candlesticks.

In 1530, at the age of forty-seven, Babur fell ill and died in India. Recalling the pleasures of his time in Afghanistan, the dying monarch asked to be laid to rest in his favorite garden of the ten that he had built in and around Kabul. For nine years, he remained buried at Agra, but his faithful Afghan wife, Bibi Mubarika Yusufzai, brought him back to his beloved city. Bagh-e-Babur (the Gardens of Babur) in Kabul is his final resting-place.

Over the next two hundred years the Mughals contested Afghan territory with the Shia Safavid dynasty of Iran in the west, and the Khanate of Bukhara in the north. By the beginning of the eighteenth century, however, all sides had surrendered to local Pashtun rulers. The tribes of the Hindu Kush were growing stronger and better able to exploit the waning power of their distant rulers.

The Durrani Empire

In Iran the Safavids were displaced by the Afsharids, a dynasty of Turkic origin from Khorasan. After the assassination in 1747 of its founder, Nadir Shah, the Afsharid Empire fell apart. Realizing the opportunity of a throne, Nadir Shah's former treasurer, the twenty-five-year-old Ahmad Shah, rallied the Pashtun tribes in Kandahar and

called for a *Loya Jirga* (grand assembly) to select a leader from among them. On being chosen, he adopted the title Durr-i-Durrani (Pearl of Pearls) and began a short period of rule in Afghanistan. This event marked the emergence of Afghanistan as an independent political entity.

From his new capital in Kandahar, Ahmad Shah Durrani went on to capture Kabul. Having consolidated his power in Afghanistan, he advanced on Mughal Delhi, which he sacked in 1757. When invited to accept the throne of India, he declined and returned to Kandahar, leaving a puppet Mughal emperor in control but retaining the lands west of the Indus. A short poem written by Ahmad Shah at this time reveals his intentions:

I will conquer countless lands
And revive the memory of Sher Shah;
But I cannot forget the fascinating orchards of
*   my motherland.*
When I think of the mountain peaks of my country,
I forget the throne of Delhi.

Ahmad Shah's control of northern India was soon challenged by the Hindu Maratha Confederacy, which he defeated in the battle of Panipat in 1761. Later he would have to subdue Sikh uprisings in Punjab and rebellions in the north. His genius lay in his ability to inspire his obstinate, volatile countrymen with a sense of national identity. Though the empire fragmented after his death in 1772, Ahmad Shah "Baba" is remembered as the Father of Afghanistan, and the founder of the Afghan nation.

The Great Game and the "Iron Amir"
Ahmad Shah's reign was followed by years of great turbulence. It was not until 1826 that Dost Mohammad Khan, founder of the Barakzai dynasty, was able to exert sufficient control and restore order, declaring himself *Amir*. Dost Mohammad

was the leader of the Pashtun Muhammadzai tribe and ruled at the onset of the Anglo–Russian power struggle known as "The Great Game." This was a century-long

contest for domination of Central Asia, in which Afghanistan played a key role. As Russia expanded south toward the Amu Darya (Oxus), Britain was intent on protecting India, the jewel in the crown of its empire.

When, in the first Anglo–Afghan War of 1839–42, Britain tried to bring Afghanistan under direct rule, it suffered a great defeat. After Britain's second attempt in 1878–80, Afghanistan lost much territory and control of its external affairs.

1929, King Amanullah abdicated and left Kabul by Rolls-Royce for Kandahar, leaving the throne to his brother Inayatullah, who followed him into exile three days later in a British plane.

Habibullah Kalakani, the son of a Tajik water carrier, known as Bacha Saqao, seized power and kept the throne for nine chaotic months. But Mohammed Nadir Shah, a Pashtun general and former minister of war, gathered his tribal army and returned to rescue Kabul, executing Saqao. With Nadir Shah a new era began in Afghanistan, but four years later he was assassinated by a teenage Hazara student. His nineteen-year-old son, Zahir Shah, became Afghanistan's last king in 1933.

During his forty-year reign, King Zahir Shah introduced a series of cautious and moderate

reforms that modernized Afghanistan and made it politically stable. Under the "New Democracy," which lasted from 1964 to 1973, he developed a new constitution that left power in the hands of the monarchy, gave judicial power to religious leaders, and created an economic framework that allowed free enterprise. During this time intellectuals and Afghan civil society enjoyed greater freedom. Women began to enter the workplace, and the wearing of the veil was made voluntary. The sixties brought about a more modern and secular Afghanistan.

But in July 1973, King Zahir Shah's cousin, the prime minister, Prince Muhammad Daoud, staged a coup and declared Afghanistan a republic with himself as president. Under his rule, Afghanistan underwent major changes in its domestic and foreign policies. Daoud's foreign policy was steered by two main principles: to improve relations with the Soviet Union without sacrificing economic aid from the United States, and to pursue the "Pashtunistan" issue by every possible means. Foreign relations between Afghanistan and Pakistan had been strained since Pakistan was formed in 1947, and much of the difficulty was linked to the creation of the Durand Line.

Afghan Communism

Daoud's ties with the Soviet Union deteriorated gradually during his presidency. By 1978, he had achieved little of the economic progress he had set out to accomplish and lost most of his political support. Kabul was now a hotbed of political ideology. In April 1978, soldiers stormed the presidential palace and killed him in a coup—the Saur Revolution—led by the Communist People's Democratic Party of Afghanistan (PDPA), which was itself riven by factionalism. The leaders of one faction, Parcham (the banner), were expelled while the other faction, the Khalq (the masses), headed by Noor Mohammed Taraki, took power. The Communist Democratic Republic of Afghanistan lasted until 1987, when the country was renamed the Republic of Afghanistan.

The Khalq's Marxist reforms soon sparked major uprisings in the countryside.

While the Soviet Union increased aid to Taraki's regime, the United States actively supported the Afghan rebel groups. Fearing the Americans would take advantage of the escalating chaos, the Soviet Union replaced Taraki with Party rival Hafizzulah Amin, and began to consider military support. In December 1979, Soviet leader Leonid Brezhnev sent in the Red Army, killed Amin, and installed Babrak Karmal, head of the Parcham faction, as the country's new president. A new "Great Game" had begun.

The "Afghan Vietnam" and *Jihad*
The presence of the Red Army on Afghan soil had already ignited a national uprising. Russian bombing of villages claimed nearly a million Afghan lives, attracting worldwide condemnation. As the Jihadi resistance grew (a religious term, *jihad* means both an inner spiritual and an outer physical struggle), support came from the Mujahideen— fighters from the mountain areas under the command of tribal leaders who also headed Islamist

political parties that ranged from radical to
moderate. The Mujahideen were mainly funded
by the United States and Saudi Arabia to fight a
nationalist war against the Soviet Union. Viewed as
outlaws by their Soviet enemy, these unorganized
guerrilla warriors were seen as freedom fighters
by the Reagan administration in the United States.

The United States was determined to turn
Afghanistan into "a Vietnam" for the Russians,
and poured in money and weapons to arm the
opposition through the ISI, the Pakistani secret
intelligence services. Anti-Communist support also
came from Britain, other Western countries, and
Islamic nations such as Saudi Arabia, wishing to
assist the "holy fighters" of the Afghan Mujahideen.

The war cost the Soviets an estimated 15,000
deaths and proved a significant catalyst for the
collapse of the Soviet Union. The inability to crush
the US-backed Mujahideen compelled Moscow to
announce a unilateral withdrawal in 1989 and to
leave Afghanistan after a decade-long embroilment.

The Geneva Accords of 1988, negotiated between
the United States and the Soviet Union, were
intended to end the war. Instead, they left the
Afghan government in ruins. The war had caused
the deaths of more than a million Afghans, mainly
civilians; millions more had fled abroad as refugees,
many over the borders into Iran and Pakistan.

The Civil War of 1992

As the new Russian president Mikhail Gorbachev
prepared to withdraw Russian forces from
Afghanistan, Dr. Najibullah, director of the state

intelligence department (KHAD), became general secretary of the PDPA and, in 1987, replaced Karmal as president.

Najibullah attempted to pursue a policy of national reconciliation, calling for a six-month ceasefire to initiate talks with the opposition groups. Although he was prepared to put aside differences with the resistance and allow Islam a greater role, the Mujahideen rejected his proposals outright. Instead, they demanded his departure as the price for joining a joint interim government. In 1992 Najibullah agreed to hand over power to an interim government as part of a United Nations plan to end the thirteen-year-old civil strife.

The country, now renamed the Islamic State of Afghanistan, descended into civil war. Among the leaders of the warring factions were Ahmad Shah Massoud, an ethnic Tajik; Gulbuddin Hekmatyar, a Pashtun; and Abdul Rashid Dostum, an Uzbek. Despite several temporary alliances, struggles among the armed groups continued until a new group emerged—the Taliban, a fundamentalist Islamic militia that gained control of most of the country in 1996.

The Rise of the Taliban and 9/11
From being at the heart of the Cold War, Afghanistan simply dropped off the map and became fragmented. Corrupt, violent, regional warlords reduced the country to ruins. America lost interest, forgetting the billions of dollars it had spent financing the different factions. In the fall of 1996,

Taliban forces advanced from Kandahar through a belt of Pashtun villages and entered the gates of Kabul, a city with no defenders. One of their first acts was to kill the former president, Najibullah, who had been sheltering in the UN compound since his resignation in 1992.

With support from elements in Pakistan, the Taliban launched a military campaign aimed at imposing rigid Islamic rule. Over the next five years, they introduced punishments as severe as public execution of those found guilty. Men were required to grow beards and women had to wear the *burqa*, or full veil. The Taliban banned art and cultural activities, and prohibited young girls from going to school.

Around this time a wealthy Saudi, Osama bin Laden, who had funded and trained Arab Mujahideen during the Soviet occupation, renewed his support of the Taliban. When in 2001 al-Qaeda attacked the World Trade Center in New York City and the Pentagon buildings in Washington, DC, the United States demanded that the Taliban hand him over and disband his bases in Afghanistan. When their leader, Mullah Mohammed Omar, refused to oblige, the Americans launched "Operation Enduring Freedom," in which US and British special forces allied with the anti-Taliban Northern Alliance, consisting mainly of the Tajik forces of Ahmad Shah Massoud and the Uzbek forces of Abdul Rashid Dostum. More than 12,000 bombs were dropped in Afghanistan in just a few weeks, and the Taliban were driven from power.

Rebuilding a Nation with an Uncertain Future
The process of rebuilding Afghanistan began in 2001. Afghan leaders in exile signed the Bonn Agreement, forming an interim government under the leadership of Hamid Karzai. In 2004, a popular vote elected him president of the Islamic Republic of Afghanistan and a new constitution was ratified.

After 2006, the NATO-led International Security Force (ISAF) took over responsibility for defense from the US-led coalition in certain parts of the country. Predictions of the Taliban's downfall proved to be premature. Working from safe havens in Pakistan, the extremists regrouped and came back with a vengeance.

Though billions of dollars in foreign aid have poured into the country, corruption, the distorting effects of the "War on Terror," and a resurgent opium trade have left Afghanistan's economy vulnerable and its security uncertain. By 2014, NATO-led forces will have left Afghanistan. The immediate future is hard to predict. In a country that has known nothing but war for over forty ears, the assumption is that it will just continue.

A few months before his death, Dr. Najibullah, exiled in the UN compound in Kabul, engaged himself in translating Peter Hopkirk's book *The Great Game* into Pashto, his mother tongue. He told a visitor, "Afghans keep making the same mistake."

GOVERNMENT AND POLITICS

Afghanistan's 2004 constitution established the country as an Islamic Republic. The president, who is head of state and commander-in-chief of the armed forces, and two vice presidents are elected for five-year terms and are eligible for a second term. The president appoints twenty-five cabinet ministers, who are approved by the National Assembly.

The National Assembly is the legislature. It is the highest elected representative body and consists of two houses. The Wolesi Jirga (the House of the People, or Lower House), with 249 seats, is the more powerful house. Members are elected on a provincial basis and serve a five-year term; women must be represented by at least sixty-four delegates. The Wolesi Jirga is responsible for proposing and ratifying laws as well as approving the actions of the president and his veto powers. A two-thirds majority in the Wolesi Jirga can override a presidential veto.

The Meshrano Jirga (the House of Elders, or Upper House), with 102 seats, represents public figures and experts appointed by provincial and district councils as well as the president. It passes laws, approves budgets, and ratifies treaties that are then finally approved by the Wolesi Jirga.

Afghanistan's independent judiciary is headed by the Stera Mahkama (the Supreme Court). Judges are appointed by the president for ten-year terms and are approved by the Wolesi Jirga.

Political parties in Afghanistan are many in number and in a state of flux, with leaders jockeying for position and creating new parties. Ordinary Afghans are more concerned about the presence of warlords and private militia leaders in the Afghan parliament. Many parts of the country are still outside the reach of the government, and in these areas local warlords continue to hold sway over their communities. For most Afghans, the notorious warlords are corrupt and a threat to their daily lives.

Local Government

The country is divided into thirty-four provinces, or *wilayats*, with each province having its own capital and a provincial administration. Each province is further divided into smaller provincial districts, each of which is represented by a district governor. Provincial governors are appointed by the president, and district governors are chosen by the provincial governors. There are also provincial councils, which are elected through direct and general elections for a period of four years.

THE ECONOMY

The Afghan economy has always been based on agriculture and animal husbandry. The country is famous for producing some of the finest fresh and dried fruits. The production of wheat and cereal is another mainstay.

From an economic perspective, Afghanistan is one of the poorest and least developed countries in the world. Being landlocked, it depends hugely on its neighbors for transiting goods into and out of the country. Years of war and conflict have crippled its financial markets and periodically forced the economy into a state of collapse. Widespread

corruption is rampant in the government, and while the foreign aid pie has grown, the incentives to misuse and steal funds have doubled.

A significant part of the economy depends on the drug trade. The country is the world's leading opiate producer, supplying over 90 percent of the global crop. Despite the expensive and aggressive campaign to eradicate opium poppy cultivation, Afghan farmers prefer the easy cash crop to legal traditional crops, which do not bring them enough money.

On hold so far are Afghanistan's huge untapped deposits of oil, gas, lithium, copper, gold, iron ore, and other minerals—estimated at over 1 trillion US dollars, which could transform its economy. With virtually no mining industry in place, this may take decades. In the meantime many Afghans continue to suffer from shortages of housing, electricity, clean water, and medical care. At a time of growing despair about the immediate future, however, the vast potential of the country's natural resources make it a prize worth fighting for, and could deliver great prosperity to the Afghan people if criminality and weak governance could be overcome.

chapter **two**

VALUES &
ATTITUDES

THE NATIONAL PSYCHE

Afghans have a passionate sense of belonging to their homeland. Over the millennia, a diversity of peoples have come to this land and influenced its inhabitants, culture, and language, creating a patchwork of ethnicities and tribes. But as history has shown, at various points, when it came to resisting foreign interference these diverse groups were able to set aside their differences and forge a uniquely Afghan identity.

National pride is an unmistakable trait of the Afghan people. Individuals consciously cling to their national identity because it is the one thing that unites all Afghans, irrespective of their political views, ethnic differences, and whether they live inside Afghanistan or in the diaspora.

Down the ages, conflicts have been an inseparable factor in shaping the national psyche, and the recent decades of war have fractured many traditions and ties to the land. For most Afghans, the future of their country still looks insecure. However, among the younger generation, there is a renewed sense of unity for their *khaak* (soil, land, nation, home). Across the country, national sporting and civil society initiatives are also forging ties among the youth and helping them to put aside their differences.

Because of the ever-changing political situation, making generalizations about this country is a risky affair. The simple, two-dimensional international perception of Afghanistan as a fragmented nation, however, ignores the depth and richness of Afghan society.

SOCIAL CUSTOMS

There are many shared values and unwritten codes of conduct that govern interpersonal relations in Afghanistan. These rules have been the backbone of Afghan communities for centuries, through invasions, occupations, and tyrannical rule. References to such ideals are found in literature and folklore, around the themes of *wafadari* (loyalty), *dosti* (friendship), *sadaqat* (honesty), *imandari* (integrity), *ghayrat* (courage), and *namus* (honor).

These values are characteristic of Afghan society and are not taken lightly. Most Afghans are very conscious of their behavior, which may positively or negatively affect the status of themselves, their family, and their tribe.

Pashtunwali

One of the oldest and most prominent codes of ethics is the tribal law of *Pashtunwali*. Dating back to the pre-Islamic era, it means "the way of the Pashtuns," or the code of life, and refers to the traditions of the Pashtun people. Among the tribes, these unwritten rules of behavior have been passed down orally from generation to generation and are held as sacrosanct. Every Pashtun is expected to abide by the principles and age-old customs of *Pashtunwali*. Violating the code will bring dishonor and shame not just to an individual but also to the entire tribe or community.

A key concept in *Pashtunwali* is *melmastia* (hospitality), referring to generosity in welcoming a visitor. It is said that a Pashtun will never sacrifice his honor, but to give away his belongings is nothing exceptional. Pashtuns will go to great lengths to show their hospitality by providing food, shelter, and even *panah* (protection) without expecting anything in return. A guest is regarded as a gift from God, and, while in the care and company of a host, should not be harmed. This can even go as far as offering sanctuary to one's enemy.

The protection of a guest derives from another concept of the moral code known as *nanawatai* (asylum). This is a famous ritual of forgiveness offered to the wrongdoer who admits guilt by entering the home of the offended party. A Pashtun is obliged to accept *nanawatai* because the person performing it repents of his mistake. Once the ritual has been accepted, the feud is ended and no revenge can be taken. Any other behavior would dishonor the code.

Contrary to this practice is another tenet of *Pashtunwali* referred to as *badal* (vengeance, justice, or revenge). It obligates a person to avenge an insult and retaliate against anyone who harms him or a family member. Offenses against one's *zan* (woman), *zar* (wealth), or *zamin* (land) are the most common, and the only acceptable form of defending one's honor is revenge.

A popular proverb says, "A Pashtun took his vengeance after a hundred years, and said that he was in a hurry." Such disputes may involve entire tribes and can last generations until revenge is taken or a *jirga* (council) of elders is able to mediate a solution.

Though there are other codes that govern the Pashtun way of life, like *sabat* (loyalty), *imandari* (righteousness), and *tureh* (bravery), probably the most significant of them all is maintaining *nang* and *namus* (honor to oneself and to women). The responsibility of a Pashtun man is to defend his home and the women of his family against threats from outsiders. Women are normally secluded and play a passive role in Pashtun society. Though they cannot acquire honor in their own right, they can lose it through misbehavior or violence upon them. An attack on a woman, either physical or verbal, is seen as an attack on a man's honor. And, according to the concept of *namus*, it must be avenged.

A person who represents these values of *Pashtunwali* and does his utmost to abide by them is respectfully called *ghairatmand*. He is a man who has courage, strength, and pride—the embodiment of the ideal Pashtun.

Much has changed in Afghanistan since these ancient customs and habits were formalized in 1747. In recent decades, this code has been undermined by war. The West often interprets its principles as tribal extremism, while radicalization and the rise of Islamism have shifted power within the tribe from the elderly to the men with guns. For Pashtuns, however, the customary law continues to define their identity and tribal spirit.

MEHMAN NAWAZI: THE ROLE OF HOSPITALITY

In Afghanistan, the act of extending hospitality and invitations to friends and strangers is called *mehman nawazi.* As in many other Islamic countries, hospitality is a cherished tradition of Afghan culture and is common to all ethnic groups. Despite the harsh realities of everyday life, Afghans pride themselves on their hospitality. Sharing a meal or a cup of green tea is a way to cement a friendship, and if an Afghan extends an invitation, it should be readily accepted.

Afghan social activity centers largely on food. The tradition of hospitality involves visitors' being given the best the family has to offer, which means generous quantities of food and elaborate care in its preparation. When families invite relatives, friends, or guests, they spend considerable time cooking a sumptuous meal to express their *mehman nawazi.*

When dining in the home of an Afghan, don't refuse more food when it is offered to you. Instead, eat slowly, as your plate will be continuously refilled. No matter how much you eat, you'll hear, "But you haven't eaten enough!" One is never left hungry in the home of an Afghan! (See Chapter 4.)

Afghans see the act of welcoming a visitor as a way to express their respect and goodwill, and receiving praise for it is a sign of honor. They don't expect gifts in return for hospitality, but they appreciate them nevertheless. A box of sweets or chocolates, a souvenir, or an item for the home will make a good present. Gifts should be small enough for the host's *mehman nawazi* and company to serve as a reciprocal gesture, and should not outdo the hospitality of the host.

THE CONCEPT OF TIME

Afghans have a much more relaxed attitude to timekeeping than Westerners, and may strike the visitor as being casual or unpunctual. There is a complex system of calendars, however (see page 68). Both the sun and the moon are important aspects of time in Muslim culture. Holidays are regulated by the lunar cycles and prayers are fixed according to the position of the sun.

RELIGION

Religion has played a significant role at different times of Afghan history, from the early concept of a supreme deity as expressed in Zoroastrianism, to the Hellenistic pantheon, and the social and artistic influences of the Buddhist period. Afghanistan was not always religiously homogeneous, and many beliefs left their imprint on Afghan society before Islam arrived in 642 CE and spread throughout the country.

Islam in Daily Life

Today in Afghanistan, 99 percent of the population are Muslim and adhere to various branches of the Islamic faith. The overwhelming majority, estimated at more than  80 percent of the population, belong to the Sunni branch of Islam. The remaining minority are Shia Muslims, predominantly Hazaras. Non-Muslims make up about 1 percent of the population. These include Christians, Jews (a former carpet trader, who now looks after the synagogue in Kabul, is believed to be the last remaining Jew in the country), Sikhs, Hindus, Bahais, and Parsees.

Being a Muslim is a fundamental part of being an Afghan. Many view it as a religion that unifies people because it emphasizes faith over ethnicity in a mostly Muslim country. It also plays an essential role in providing daily moral, ethical, and social guidance.

Because Islam is a way of life, it functions as a code of social behavior, too. But just because someone is Westernized and liberal, it doesn't mean that their religion is not an important part of their identity. Similarly, it would be wrong to assume that a devout individual, possibly a turbaned cleric, is hostile to the West.

A *madhhab* is a Muslim school of law or religious jurisprudence. In Afghanistan, most Sunnis follow the Hanafi school of jurisprudence, which is compatible with local traditions, customs, and cultures. Religious observances punctuate the rhythm of each day. The Hanafi school puts a great emphasis on the role of reason and allows for intellectual flexibility in the interpretation of the Quran. Other *madhhabs* are the Shafi'i, Hanbali, Maliki, and Zahiri.

Muslims express their faith through the core practices known as the Five Pillars of Islam. These pillars represent the central obligations required of every adult Muslim who is able to observe them.

THE FIVE PILLARS OF ISLAM

Shahda Reciting the Muslim profession of faith
Salat Performing the ritual prayers five times a day
Zakat Giving alms to benefit the needy
Sawm Fasting during the month of Ramazan (Ramadan)
Hajj Pilgrimage to Mecca

Mosques, Mystics, and Shrines

Muslims are required to pray five times daily—after sunrise, at mid-morning, at noon, in the afternoon, and at sunset. They can pray alone or in a group. In

Afghanistan the *masjid* (mosque) is an important place of worship, but it also serves other purposes, for example as a place for local meetings, a schoolroom for traditional Islamic teaching, and a center for religious festivities and gatherings. You will find at least one *masjid* in every Afghan village, town, or neighborhood.

Though not obligatory, the central Friday mosque service of weekly communal prayers is attended by the general public. During Ramazan (Ramadan), the month of fasting, business in the markets and offices falls off considerably because an Afghan Muslim fasts every day of the month, from sunrise to sunset (see Chapter 3). A visit to the mosque during a holiday such as Eid will give you a sense of the importance of religious belief to Afghans.

In villages and towns, local religious leaders are called *mullahs*. They conduct the Friday sermon and prayers; officiate at rituals associated with births, marriages, and deaths; teach the doctrines

WHEN VISITING A MOSQUE

- Dress conservatively and behave modestly. Women do not normally visit mosques. On certain religious occasions when they can visit, they must have only their face, hands, and feet showing. Scarves should cover the head completely, including the hair.
- Before entering, remove your shoes; there may be a designated area to leave them.
- Foreigners should ask for permission before entering a mosque.
- Do not smoke in the vicinity of a mosque.
- Speak softly to avoid interrupting worshipers in prayer.
- Do not walk in front of people who are praying. The space immediately in front of a person praying is considered sacred, as it faces toward the direction of Mecca.

of Islam; and are often called upon to provide advice for social and personal problems. In the more remote parts of Afghanistan, local mullahs can be exceedingly powerful and influential in their communities.

Islamic mysticism and holy men have long been considered an integral part of the culture. Afghanistan is commonly known as "the home of Sufi saints," with more than 1,300 years of Sufi influence. The word Sufi is derived from *suf*, the Arabic word for wool, and refers to the woolen robes worn by early mystics. People in general respect the local saints, called *pirs*, and believe they possess *karamat*—a spiritual power that allows Sufi masters to perform acts of generosity and impart blessings. Cities like Herat and Ghazni are among the most important centers of Sufism, and *ziyarats*, or Sufi shrines, are popular pilgrimage sites all over the country.

Shrines also mark the final resting place of a *shaheed*, or fallen hero, a revered religious teacher, or sacred relics such as a hair of the Prophet Muhammad. The Shrine of Hazrat Ali in Mazar-e-Sharif is revered throughout Afghanistan, and both Shia and Sunni pilgrims from across the country come to pay their respects. Women, in particular, are devoted to activities associated with shrines. Many carry amulets (*taweez*) to ward off the evil eye.

Religious Tolerance
Though the constitution of Afghanistan permits followers of other religions to exercise their faith, in practice the right to religious freedom is

limited. Under Sharia law, the moral and religious code of Islam, converting from Islam to another religion is a punishable act and could even lead to the death penalty.

In a population that is almost entirely Sunni Muslim, minority groups face incidents of intolerance. At various times, the Shia communities have been persecuted for their beliefs. During the years under Taliban rule, the Shias of the Hazara ethnic minority became a target for hostility and harassment. The Taliban imposed a particularly fanatical and rigid variation of Islam on the country, to which many conservative groups were sympathetic. Hindus and Sikhs were made to wear a yellow badge on their clothing to identify them as non-Muslim citizens of Afghanistan.

Though the Taliban enforced these oppressive laws when in power, they are far removed from the interpretation of Islam followed by most Afghans. The Muslims of Afghanistan are tolerant of other religions; however, they don't stand for criticisms of Islam. For foreigners, it would be best to avoid religious discussions.

Jihad, Islam, and Religious Fundamentalism

The Soviet occupation of Afghanistan was a significant period in Afghanistan's recent history. The war of religion and nationalism transformed people's perspectives in the fight against foreign domination. The Mujahideen—the resistance in the war against the Soviets and the Kabul regime— mobilized people to fight for their country by using the culture of *jihad*.

The term *jihad* means to struggle, and refers to a holy war in defense of one's homeland, honor, and religion. According to *jihad*, those who die fighting for these values are called *shaheed* (martyrs). Not surprisingly, in the course of Afghan history, individuals and leaders have interpreted the concept of *jihad* differently according to their understanding of Islam.

By 1992, the Mujahideen had gained ground. The birth of the Islamic State of Afghanistan was a distinct break in the country's history, for religious leaders had never before exercised state power. It was also the start of a civil war.

The Mujahideen could not establish a united government, and many of the factions—supported by interested outside parties—began to fight each other for power in and around Kabul. After several years of devastating civil war, the Taliban vowed to restore peace in Afghanistan and bring in a "pure" Islamic state. Between 1996 and 2001, the Taliban emerged as a power in the land and effectively ruled most parts of the country.

The term "Taliban" refers to students of religious studies, and the typical Talib was a student of a Pakistani *madrassa* (religious school) who lacked formal education in the history of Islam and of Afghanistan. Many were strangers to the modern sciences, to arts and philosophy, and to the politics of the twenty-first century. The Afghan public supported the Taliban until they began to enforce their strict interpretation of Islam. By introducing a repressive form of Sharia law, the Taliban closed girls' schools, confined women to their homes, and banned all forms of entertainment. Violation of their rules led to beatings, public persecution, and executions.

The strength of the Islamist movement in Afghanistan today rests largely on its military capabilities and on the support and guidance of its external political backers. Islamic fundamentalism itself is not a popular movement in Afghanistan, but it has, at different times, played a critical role in Afghan politics and society.

SOCIAL HIERARCHIES

Afghan society is hierarchical, and is structured primarily along regional, religious, tribal, and ethnic lines. An individual's kinship is defined by *qaum* (ancestral and tribal lineage) and *manteqa* (the place or region from which the individual originates).

Within the Afghan social order there are great differences in wealth and status. At the top of the social ladder are the elite, who come mainly from well-connected landowning and wealthy business families, and govern the country. Their members can also be found in top positions in the state apparatus, serving as army generals, ministers, judges, and governors. They also hold leading positions in the private sector, and work for international organizations based outside Afghanistan. A significant number have studied abroad and have had access to higher education.

The elite of the rural areas are mainly the tribal chiefs, who are less sophisticated and typically lack an educational background or exposure to other societies. However, they understand the politics of their local communities and can easily exercise influence over their people. The largest social segment of the country's population is the peasantry. Unlike their urban counterparts, they live a very modest life with limited contact with communities outside their own.

Within the pecking order of the ethnic groups, Pashtuns occupy the higher end of the social spectrum and make up the merchant class as well as filling most government and civil service jobs. Tajiks also serve as traders and craftsmen, while the Hazara community is generally at the bottom of the employment scale, doing menial labor.

Afghan business culture dictates a strict hierarchical structure in which leaders separate themselves from the group and power is wielded from the top. There is usually only one key decision maker—the most senior person in a company. Subordinates represent the business during meetings, but do not have the authority to make decisions (see Chapter 8).

FAMILY, GENDER, AND *ZAN*

The family is the single most important institution in Afghan society, and is a strictly private domain. Family ties and honor are sacred among Afghans, and determine a family's status in society. The family structure is patriarchal, with authority vested in men (see Chapter 5). Life as an Afghan *zan* (woman), on the other hand, is an enormous challenge. Women and girls, as a whole, experience varying degrees of gender oppression, both political and social.

Throughout Afghanistan's modern history, the status of women has been used as an indicator of social change. Over the years, many women have found themselves caught between Western concepts of modernization and Afghanistan's extremist, traditional codes of culture. In the 1970s, women's rights were enshrined in the national constitution, which enabled many to study and work as nurses, doctors, and teachers in the public domain. But three decades later, under Taliban rule, women were oppressed and essentially put under house arrest. Afghanistan today remains a country where women's rights are still under threat, violence against women is increasing, and the risk of acid attacks has even threatened the lives of girls going to school.

Though a more democratic view of women's rights has begun to take hold—founded in the country's new 2004 constitution and promoted by

the newly created Ministry of Women's Affairs—
many Afghan women resort to suicide, some by self-
immolation, to escape their misery.

There is, however, a better life and economic
opportunities for those in the cities and towns.
Women have run for office, been appointed to
government posts, and become more involved in

Afghan society; some operate
their own businesses while
others have been recruited into
the air force and the Afghan
national police. Many women's
groups are also reaching out to
support women through civil
society initiatives. However, with
a fluctuating history of women's
rights, there is immense concern
about what the future holds for
Afghan women.

ATTITUDES TOWARD OTHERS

Historically, the country has always been impacted
by unwelcome external influences. International
players have repeatedly shown a short attention span
with regard to Afghanistan, but Afghans feel it is
their regional neighbors who have permanent
interests and are a potential source of instability.

Despite sharing a common border, ethnic group,
and religion, Afghanistan and Pakistan have had an
uneasy relationship. Many Afghans feel a palpable
sense of animosity toward Pakistan, viewing it with
great suspicion. The status of the Durand Line is a

matter of historic importance for the Afghan people and remains a bone of contention. Afghans lay claim to a large part of northwestern Pakistan, which they believe the British stole, dividing the Pashtun land.

Afghans are quite passionate and vocal about Pakistan's true intentions. In recent years, ties between the two countries have become more strained after the Afghan government began openly accusing Pakistan of harboring and aiding militant groups. Many feel that Pakistan is interfering in Afghan affairs in order to keep the country in a state of conflict and so to wield influence in it.

Although you hardly ever hear a good word about Pakistan, you rarely hear a bad one about its great rival, India. Walk through the markets in Kabul and you soon lose count of the number of places selling Indian music and movies. Afghanistan has always had a kinder image of India. A friendly country, it is also one of the biggest donors, having pledged money for projects ranging from road construction to the building of the Afghan parliament.

Relations between Afghanistan and its other neighbor, Iran, have been grim in modern times. Iran accepted millions of refugees during the Soviet occupation and the subsequent civil war and Taliban takeover. Iranians show less respect now for Afghan refugees and migrants living in their country. Though Afghans carry out menial jobs that no Iranian would be seen doing, they are often paid the most miserly of wages and are ill treated. In recent years, Iran has been forcibly deporting some of them back to Afghanistan, and their plight has become a source of tension between the two countries.

chapter three

CUSTOMS & TRADITIONS

Afghanistan's diverse calendars of events reflect its ancient past, its Islamic heritage, and the modern era. Religious and national holidays are popular occasions, and make a break from the uncertainty and difficulties of everyday life.

THE CALENDARS

Daily life is shaped by three different calendars: the traditional solar calendar (Hejrah-e shamsi), the Islamic lunar calendar (Hejrah-e qamari), and the Gregorian (Western) calendar.

The Afghans and members of the expatriate community who are working in international development organizations, foreign companies, and diplomatic missions primarily use the Western calendar. Foreign visitors, however, will find it more valuable to plan their meetings and social activities with the help of the local calendars, which determine religious and national festivals.

The official calendar in Afghanistan is the traditional solar calendar, which begins on the vernal equinox. All national holidays and administrative issues are fixed according to this calendar. However, the dates of the important

Muslim festivals, most notably the fasting month of Ramazan (Ramadan), are determined by the Islamic lunar calendar. In both the traditional solar and lunar calendars the years are counted from the time of the Prophet Muhammad's flight from Mecca to Medina in 622 CE.

The lunar year is eleven days shorter than that of the Western calendar. Each month begins with the sighting of the new moon. In Afghanistan, religious officials have the authority to declare the sighting, so while future Islamic holidays can be estimated, the precise dates are always in doubt until a few days prior to the start of the month.

Thus in 2014, for example, you might hear and see people in Afghanistan talk about the year being 1393, according to the traditional solar calendar. The start of the Afghan New Year is celebrated by a pre-Islamic festival called Nowroz, marking the vernal equinox around March 20. Thus, the Afghan year between March 2014 and March 2015 is 1393, the year between March 2015 and March 2016 is 1394, and so on. All government and commercial business is done according to this system, although Afghans are aware that the years are counted differently from other systems.

If you are spending any length of time in Afghanistan, knowledge of the traditional calendar will be essential in coping with daily life. In the Afghan solar calendar, the twelve months are named after the twelve constellations of the zodiac, in both Dari and Pashto. The names of the months are listed below, starting with Hamal (in Dari) or Worai (in Pashto), the first month of the New Year.

Afghan months end around the twentieth day of a Western month.

Month Dari	Pashto	Western/Gregorian
(Hejrah-e shamsi)	(Hejrah-e shamsi)	
1 Hamal (Aries)	Worai	March–April
2 Saur (Taurus)	Ghwayai	April–May
3 Jauza (Gemini)	Ghbargolay	May–June
4 Saratan (Cancer)	Changaakh/Changaash	June–July
5 Asad (Leo)	Zmarai	July–August
6 Sonbola (Virgo)	Wazhai/Waghai	August–Sept.
7 Mizan (Libra)	Tala	Sept.–October
8 Aqrab (Scorpio)	Laram	October–Nov.
9 Qaus (Sagittarius)	Lendai	Nov.–Dec.
10 Jadi (Capricorn)	Marghomai	Dec.–January
11 Dalw (Aquarius)	Salwaagha	January–February
12 Hut (Pisces)	Kab	February–March

The days of the week are: Shambe (Saturday), Yak-shambe (Sunday), Do-shambe (Monday), Se-shambe (Tuesday), Char-shambe (Wednesday), Panj-shambe (Thursday), and Jhumah (Friday). It's worth noting that the week begins on Saturday and ends on Friday, the day of rest.

RELIGIOUS FESTIVALS AND NATIONAL HOLIDAYS
Greater and Smaller Eid
The major religious festivals of Eid-e-Qurban (elsewhere called Eid ul-Azha, or Greater Eid) and Eid-ul-Fitr (Smaller Eid) are celebrated across the country.

On Eid-e-Qurban, or the Feast of Sacrifice, families mark the occasion by slaughtering a goat or a sheep in commemoration of the Prophet Abraham's readiness to obey God even to the point of sacrificing his son, Ismail. At God's command, Abraham spared his son and was provided with a lamb to sacrifice in his stead.

In the days ahead of this holy day, large numbers of people throng the markets to buy sacrificial animals. Those who can afford it slaughter one or more, sharing the meat with relatives and distributing it to the poor. In Afghanistan, Eid-e-Qurban lasts three days, during which the entire country effectively shuts down. The holiday takes place at the end of the Hajj season, around seventy days after the end of Ramazan.

Eid-ul-Fitr, the Smaller Eid, falls at the end of the month of Ramazan in the lunar calendar year. Ramazan is the auspicious holy month of fasting, and marks the period in which the Quran was revealed to the Prophet Muhammad. During this month, participating Muslims do not eat or drink anything from sunrise to sunset, although children, the elderly, and the pregnant are exempt. Muslims ask for forgiveness for past sins, pray, and purify themselves through self-restraint and good deeds.

While foreigners are not expected to fast, they should avoid eating, drinking, or smoking in public areas during daylight hours. Failure to do so will attract negative attention for cultural insensitivity. You will be eating in private during the day, as local shops and restaurants remain closed until sunset.

Eid-ul-Fitr is always on the same day of the lunar calendar; however, the date in the Western calendar falls around eleven days earlier each successive year. Eid may also vary from country to country, depending on the sighting of the moon.

The breaking of the fast at the end of the day during Ramazan is called Iftar. Families in the neighborhood congregate to eat, drink, and pray. As in the rest of the Muslim world, it is traditional to

 eat dates first, followed by local savory dishes such as *bolani*, a filled flat bread (see picture on page 93), kebabs, and rice.

The rituals involved in celebration of both Eids are very similar. Particularly on the first day of Eid, Afghans wear new clothes and visit their families and

friends. People greet one another with "*Eid Mubarak*" (the equivalent of "Happy Eid"). The host family welcomes the visitors and offers them tea and sweets, followed by a meal. Some friends and relatives exchange gifts, while the children receive cash presents called *Eidi.*

Nowroz, "The New Day"

The festival of Nowroz, the New Year, as we have seen, falls generally around March 20 each year. Literally meaning "the new day," Nowroz is an ancient Aryan festival that marks the vernal equinox, the exact astronomical beginning of spring. At this time it is a tradition among Afghans to forgive and forget each other's mistakes and start the New Year with a clear conscience.

On this day, Afghan families decorate their homes and wear new clothes. People visit each other at home and greet one another with

"*Nowroz Mubarak*" (Happy New Year). The women of the house prepare elaborate dishes to welcome visiting friends and family members. A popular dish called *haft mewa* is a mixture of seven dried fruits and nuts—raisins, pistachios, a dried fruit from the wild olive or oleaster tree, hazelnuts, prunes, walnuts, and almonds—that correspond to the seven elements of life, namely fire, earth, water, air, plants, animals, and humans. The dish symbolizes the beginning of spring.

Also on Nowroz farmers display their produce in Kabul and other major cities, celebrating the farmer's festival known as Jashn-e-Dehqan.

When the Taliban seized power, they declared such customs to be anti-Islamic, and prohibited people from celebrating Nowroz. In recent times, however, these events have started to be held again.

Mawlid-e Sharif
The birthday of the Prophet Muhammad is marked on the twelfth day of the month of Rabi al-Awal in the Islamic lunar calendar. Mawlid-e Sharif (known elsewhere as Mawlid al-Nabi) is an important religious day. Men visit mosques to pray and listen to the sermons eulogizing the Prophet. Women prepare dishes and give alms (*khairat*) to the poor.

Muharram

Muharram, the first month of the Islamic calendar, marks the death of the Prophet Muhammad's grandson and the third Shia Imam, Hussein, at the battle of Karbala in 680 in modern-day Iraq. To the Shia community, Imam Hussein is regarded as the true successor to the Prophet, so this month is a period of grief and sorrow for Shias. The tenth day is known as *dah-e-ashura*, and is a day of voluntary fasting. Shias gather to listen to sermons eulogizing Imam Hussein for giving his life in defense of justice and sing emotional songs lamenting his death. People weep and wail, and men flagellate themselves until they bleed. The mourning period continues for forty days, during which time Shias postpone any joyful ceremonies. Sunnis, too, observe the occasion with prayers and acts of charity. Muharram is not a celebration, so foreigners would be wrong to congratulate their Afghan friends on this holiday.

Jashn-e Afghan

Afghanistan's Independence Day on August 19 commemorates the Treaty of Rawalpindi in 1919, which confirmed the country's complete independence from Britain. This celebration of the end of the British Empire's three attempts to rule Afghanistan in the Anglo–Afghan Wars is an important national event, and is marked by the government and political groups alike. While the official celebrations take place in the Afghan Defense Ministry compound with a small military

parade, the different political groups organize meetings with speeches and discussions.

The days listed below are other public holidays in Afghanistan, when businesses and government offices are closed.

Liberation Day, February 15

This day commemorates the date of the Soviet withdrawal from Afghanistan in 1989. Political speeches are televised to stir up national feelings. Some Afghans also view the day as a religious holiday, because the end of the Soviet occupation also resulted in the end of the secular ideas of the Marxist government.

Victory Day, April 28

This date marks the end of Communist rule in Afghanistan, when the Mujahideen overthrew the country's Soviet-backed government in 1992. It is celebrated with a military parade, but with ongoing security threats the government has scaled down the event and sometimes even cancels it. An assassination attempt on President Hamid Karzai by gunmen and suicide bombers marred the festivities in 2008.

Massoud Day, September 9
This day is named after the Northern Alliance leader Ahmad Shah Massoud, who was killed in 2001 by two Arab suicide bombers posing as journalists. On this day, Afghans remember those who have been martyred.

FAMILY CEREMONIES AND TRADITIONS
Birth
Afghan families regard their children as an indispensable asset: children ensure the continuity of their lineage and support them in their old age. When a son is born, an elaborate feast is arranged, depending on the extent of the family's wealth. Some ethnic communities fire guns and beat drums to welcome the newborn baby and celebrate the occasion. The birth of a girl is not considered as important, although this is not always the case. Certain families value their offspring equally, whether they are boys or girls.

In urban areas, families celebrate *shab-e-shash* (six nights after a birth) and invite friends and relatives, who bring presents for the newborn. The mullah, the local religious leader, performs one of the first ceremonies. A popular belief is that a child is born without faith, so the mullah or an elder recites a prayer from the Quran into each ear of the child. Several other ceremonies are held over time, such as the naming ceremony, *chela guraez* (a party thrown for the mother forty days after a child's birth), and the *khat nasuri* (circumcision).

The Wedding Experience
Extravagant weddings are a highlight of modern Afghan life and an important measure of social status. Among the wealthy, lavish weddings in banqueting halls decorated with blinking neon lights have become the norm. Custom dictates that all relatives, distant members of the family, and friends be invited, and guests dress in their best suits and evening wear.

Traditionally, a line of men and women from the bride's and groom's families stands on each

side of the entrance to greet and escort the guests. When all guests have arrived, local musicians play traditional songs and contemporary hits.

The religious ceremony, the *nikah*, is held in private with a gathering of the couple's immediate families. The *nikah* is negotiated between the groom, with his representatives, and the bride's representatives before the mullah. At this time bride and groom wait in separate rooms. Once the groom has accepted the terms of the marriage, the mullah will come before the bride and ask her three times if she also accepts the marriage. Then the couple is pronounced husband and wife.

A traditional Afghan wedding usually begins in the evening and ends before midnight—or later, depending on how long the hall has been hired for. A special song, "Ahesta Boro" (meaning "Walk Slowly"), is played to welcome the bride and groom on their arrival at the banqueting hall and to mark the start of the festivities. At the end of the hall is a stage with decorated chairs, on which the bride and groom sit in state.

A number of local traditions take place in an Afghan wedding after the *nikah*, one of which is *aina moshaf*. The bride and groom are covered with a shawl, under which they read verses from the Quran and are given a mirror to view themselves for the first time as a married couple. Once the shawl is lifted, the bride and groom feed each other *malida*, a dessert made from sweet breadcrumbs, and intertwine their arms to offer each other a sip of juice.

Other traditions include painting the bride and groom's hands with henna, and cutting the wedding cake. After a sumptuous meal, toward the end of the evening, the guests and the newlyweds perform the traditional circular Afghan dance called the *Attan*.

Death and Funerals

Over the last three decades of war, the rituals surrounding death have become a common sight in the country. The Afghans follow the traditional Islamic way of burial. Muslims believe in prompt burial following a ritual cleansing of the body. Male relatives lift the bier, carrying the carefully wrapped body to the burial ground, where it is placed in the ground facing toward the *Kaaba* in Mecca. If the deceased is a woman, the ceremonies are the same, but the washing is done by a female member of the family. The body is buried as verses from the Quran are read. The

funeral service for a man is held in the mosque, and for a woman at her home. Traditionally, mourners wear black clothing for a funeral procession.

Feasts of remembrance are held every Thursday night during the mourning period, and mourners are invited to dinner and to read verses from the Quran for the dead. On the fortieth day, which is called the *chahlum*, friends and relatives join in the mourning and visit the grave to pray. Once the *chahlum* is over, there is no other formal function until the first anniversary.

FOLKLORE AND SUPERSTITIONS

In many parts of Afghanistan, people combine Muslim belief with the superstitious practices that are part of daily life. While many of these arise from religious stories and old beliefs, most are related to the fear of being cursed. There is a widespread belief in *djinns*—invisible, demon-like creatures that hide in dark places and play tricks on people. Elders will often scare children into obedience with the threat of *djinns*. Women in particular observe practices such as wearing *taweez* (amulets containing prayers), to keep *djinns* from harming them. Burning seeds of *esfand* (a common weed) on charcoal will avert the evil eye.

SOME COMMON SUPERSTITIONS

- Playing with scissors brings about a fight.
- An itchy palm brings money.
- An itchy foot will take you on a journey.
- If you bite your tongue, someone is speaking ill of you.
- A twitchy eye brings about good news.
- Whatever happens on New Year's Day will happen for the rest of the year.
- Passing salt directly to someone creates distance.
- Complimenting a person may also jinx them and bring bad luck.
- Throwing water behind a departing person will bring them good luck and a safe journey.

chapter four

MAKING FRIENDS

FRIENDSHIP

For Afghans friendship (*dosti*) is viewed as a lifelong attachment. Its enduring nature is summed up in the popular saying, "The first day you meet, you are friends. The next day you meet, you are brothers."

Afghans tend to be affectionate and expressive, and to have a deep sense of belonging. Decades of war and economic challenges have meant that life has not been easy for many, and people have learned to rely on each other. Trust and loyalty are the bedrock of a true friendship, and earning it may take time and persistence.

Friendships are highly valued and people go out of their way to meet their friends' needs and to be present and helpful during times of crisis. Many even risk life and livelihood for one another. Some of the most abiding friendships and trusting relationships are forged within the extended family. Families in Afghanistan are usually extremely close units (see Chapter 5), which draw even more closely together at times of trouble. As important are childhood friends, school classmates, and college roommates, who provide a sense of companionship and a secure bond throughout one's lifetime.

FOREIGNERS AND FRIENDSHIP

Making friends as a foreigner may seem easy in Afghanistan. Everywhere you go, people will want to engage you in conversation, find out about your country, and ask your impressions of Afghanistan. Of course, it is one thing to make acquaintances and another to make friends.

The experience of foreign intervention in Afghanistan from the nineteenth century to the present day has led Afghans to regard Westerners with a great deal of suspicion. Confronted by anti-Western rhetoric, foreigners should remember that it is a matter of politics directed at governments and not at individuals. In the streets at least, ordinary people are astonishingly ready to help if they see someone in trouble. While it pays to be street smart, as it does anywhere else, don't be wary of seemingly unprompted acts of kindness. In Afghanistan, these are often real and hide no ulterior motive.

Shopkeepers may offer you a cup of green tea, an acquaintance may invite you to his home for an authentic meal, or a fellow passenger may even quietly pay the bill for your souvenirs. However, making genuine friends as a visiting foreigner is not always this straightforward. If an Afghan considers you a friend, you have entered into a relationship that brings with it expectations that are not always anticipated by Westerners. Interactions between Afghans and foreigners can throw up a mass of cultural differences, and it is important to break these barriers with time, understanding, and effort.

There are, of course, many privileges in the life of a resident expat that ordinary Afghans are understandably bitter about. Expatriate bars and restaurants catering to the foreign community are quite hip in cities like Kabul, but with the exception of Afghanistan's upper echelon, the locals are not

allowed in. Foreigners on assignments earn several times as much as their Afghan counterparts, despite having similar qualifications. Many working for diplomatic missions, media groups, or international organizations come and go at their will, but it is the Afghans who stay and form the backbone of the operation. In a worst-case scenario, a foreigner can also leave the country very quickly, which is not an option for most Afghans.

As a visitor, if you are alert and sensitive to such issues, the experience of living and working in the country can become deeply personal. If you succeed in overcoming the barriers, a friendship made in Afghanistan is something to be treasured, and is likely to last a lifetime.

MAKING CONVERSATION
Although some have been hardened by war, the Afghans are typically warm and welcoming people. For the most part, they have a great curiosity about Westerners and foreign cultures.

Everywhere you go, people will ask you the same questions: "What is your name?" "Where are you from?" "What does your family do?" "Where do you work?" "How long have you been here?" And of course, "Do you like Afghanistan?" Afghans will not hesitate to ask about your stance when it comes to political issues. When engaging in such topics, foreigners should be well informed about local points of view and political sensitivities before sharing their opinion on Afghanistan.

Generally, Afghans have far fewer inhibitions about asking personal questions than Westerners. It is relatively normal to ask about your educational qualifications, relationship status, or family background. One of the first questions you will have to field is whether you are married. If the answer is "no," be prepared for a follow-up "*chura?*" (why?). Don't expend too much energy trying to make people understand such cultural variations. If they cannot relate at first, they still learn to respect and trust you over time. A simple rule is to be yourself! Afghans are good judges of character, and see through pretentiousness.

TABOOS

Afghans are very private in another sense, and do not like discussing marital or family problems out in the open. Sexual matters, such as dating, or sharing details of a personal relationship, are considered taboo, and it is best to avoid this subject altogether. Afghans are very sensitive about religion and in-your-face views on politics, and topics such as women's rights and equality are provocative. Any criticism of the country or culture is considered highly offensive, and it is best to end a conversation that is not culturally tolerable.

Body language, social cues, and assumptions differ so greatly from those in the West that it may be difficult for someone just entering the country to "read" certain forms of behavior without being alarmed. During your interactions with Afghans, you may notice that they talk loudly and are often indirect. Their conversations are laced with metaphors, and *zarbul masalha* (proverbs), when used, carry the weight of an entire explanation.

SOME AFGHAN PROVERBS

Zakhme shamsher jor meysha, zakhme zabaan ney. "A sword wound will heal, but not a wound from words." (People remember harsh statements longer than physical pain.)

Az yak dast sadaa bar namey-khizad. "From one hand comes no sound." (Just as one hand can't clap by itself, a person can't succeed alone; or, it is better to cooperate with others.)

Gel-e khoshk ba dewar namey chaspad. "Dry mud won't stick to a wall." (Accusations and lies with no basis won't stick and don't bother me.)

Aasman duhr, zameen sakht. "The sky is far, the earth hard." (There are no good options, and there is no escape; or, between the devil and the deep blue sea.)

Deyr ayaad, dorost aayad. "Comes late, comes right." (It is better to work slowly and well than quickly and badly; or, it is better to arrive late than never.)

GETTING STARTED

The biggest obstacle to making friends is the language. Some Afghans, especially in big cities like Kabul, speak perfect English, but in other places you may find that people's grasp of English is elementary or nonexistent. Try to learn the basic greetings, at the very least. It will endear you to almost everyone in Afghanistan and make you an instant celebrity. Dari and Pashto are the two official languages, but Dari is the one more commonly used. Afghans love to hear you try, and are very forgiving of your mistakes.

MEETING AFGHANS

It's useful to understand some of the social etiquette of the country, as it will help you to understand why Afghans act the way they do. It will also go a long way toward making you feel at home here.

Greetings

The handshake is a customary part of greeting in Afghanistan. Handshakes are used to welcome male guests, although it is more common to put your hand on your heart and bow slightly to new acquaintances and to embrace among friends.

Between women, kissing three times on the cheek is the most common form of greeting. However, men and women in Afghanistan do not express affection of any sort in public, even a simple touch of the hands. Men greet women verbally and avoid eye contact with the opposite sex. The golden rule for a Western man is to let the woman take the initiative. If in doubt, wait for the woman to extend her hand before making the same gesture.

The traditional way of saying Hello is *Salam*, although people use the full Arabic *Assalam alaykom* (May peace be with you) and the reply *Waalaykum assalam* (And peace to you also). Depending on the time of the day, you can wish someone *Sob bekhayr* (Good morning) or *Shab bekhayr* (Good evening). "Yes" in Dari is *baley*, though in colloquial speech *aan* is often used. "No" is *nakhayr*, though this is almost always shortened to *ney*.

Afghans usually start a conversation by inquiring about the other person's health and their family's welfare. It is important that you reciprocate and make the same inquiry in return. With this out of the way, you can then attack the matter at hand. The normal openings for a conversation in Dari are *Haley-tan chetor hast?* (How are you?), or just *Shoma chetor hasten?* (You well?). You might reply *Man khub-am* (I'm fine) or *Bad neystam* (I'm not bad). It will not be long before the curious ask *Nameytan chist?* (What's your name?) and *Az khojah hasten?* (Which country are you from?). You may reply *Namam —hast* (My name is —) and *Man az — hastam* (I am from —).

Many people will want to know what you think of Afghanistan, and they will be delighted by a positive answer. *Afghanistan ra dost daram* (I like Afghanistan) or *Een-mamlakat besyaar maqbool hast* (This country is very beautiful) will bring a smile to many faces.

Personal Space

You may find a great disparity between your own sense of personal space and the close proximity of both friend and stranger in Afghanistan. Expect people to infringe on your conversational comfort zone where distance is concerned. It is common to see a foreigner move away as an Afghan inches closer. On the other hand, personal space must be preserved when interacting with women, and getting too close can be interpreted as disrespecting a woman.

Saying No

Hospitality is a deeply rooted tradition in the country and is closely related to an individual's honor and reputation. Underlining the importance of courtesy in Afghan culture, hospitality extended should always be graciously accepted.

As a foreign visitor, avoid a blunt refusal of an invitation and even of a favor asked of you. A direct refusal is interpreted as rude and impolite. Instead, suggest that an effort will be made and prepare yourself to offer seemingly indefinite responses, such as *Inshallah* (God willing).

DRESS

One thing that is not necessary in Afghanistan is to dress up very much, as drawing attention to oneself is frowned upon. Religious belief has to a great extent influenced people's style of clothing. It generally stresses modesty in women, who lead largely sheltered lives under gauzy veils or shrouded long dresses, and simplicity and ease of movement for men. Women must wear the Islamic headscarf and have all bodily contours covered when in public. Men should not wear shorts, except when playing sports.

The *perahan-tonbaan* is the most recognizable garment of Afghan men; it consists of a knee-length shirt and baggy pants. A waistcoat may be worn with it. Most Afghan men wear a *patoo* (shawl) over their shoulders, along with a cap or turban.

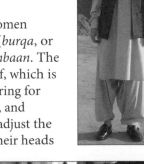

Traditional clothing for women includes the *chadar*, *chadari* (*burqa*, or full veil), and the *perahan-tonbaan*. The *chadar* is a shawl or headscarf, which is the most common head covering for women. It is not easy to wear, and women frequently have to readjust the folds in the street to ensure their heads

are properly covered. Many Afghan women continue to wear the *chadari* to be more mobile and secure.

Foreign women are strongly recommended to wear headscarves and modest clothing (see page 137), which will gain you a better reception in the country.

VISITING AN AFGHAN HOME

An invitation to an Afghan home is a great honor, and is likely to be a highlight of your trip.

When entering a family home, Afghans take off their shoes or sandals, as the floor is generally covered with carpets. The same rule applies to guests. The standard seating arrangement in the living room will be a long, narrow mattress placed directly on the carpet, running around the walls, with cushions against which to recline. Afghans, rich or poor, educated or illiterate, sit on the mattress with their legs folded, and guests are expected to do likewise. Only in a few, rich, urban households are

you likely to find Western sofas and armchairs, but even these families will maintain the tradition of having a few rooms lined with carpets, mattresses, and cushions. Male guests are received and entertained in these outer rooms with green tea and a platter of almonds, walnuts, and raisins, while visiting women will be taken to the inner sanctum, or the *zenana mahal*.

Close family members, male and female, eat their meals together, sitting on the floor. A cloth known as *dastarkhan* is spread on the carpet and the food is placed on it. When families have outside guests, the males and females will be separated for meals, but the custom of sitting on the floor to eat will still be followed.

From the Same Platter

The communal practice of sharing plates may come as a shock to outsiders. Except in some urban families, separate plates and cutlery for each person are not normally used. Food will be served on big platters, and three or four people will eat, using their fingers, from different sides of the nearest platter. A pile of naan (Afghan bread) is placed in the middle of the dastarkhan, and everyone helps themselves. Even glasses for drinking water are shared.

To prepare yourself for a more culturally rewarding experience when mingling with Afghans, there are a few tips and dos and don'ts to remember.

Wait for your host to show you where to sit, and make sure to sit cross-legged, or as comfortably as you can, but not with your legs outstretched. Ensure that your feet are tucked away, not facing toward anyone.

In conversation, remember the taboos listed above, and don't inquire from male friends and acquaintances about their wives, daughters, or any female family members. If you wish to take a photo, especially of women, ask permission first. Before departing, ask permission to leave your host's residence. When you leave, put your shoes on in a corner without turning your back on other people.

Don't use your left hand to greet or even pass something to another person. The left hand serves a specific purpose—hygiene after the use of the toilet. Don't point your finger at anyone, as this is taken as a threat or insult. Don't blow your nose, burp, or spit in public. These actions are considered rude and insulting. Winking has a sexual connotation, so it's best avoided.

As we have seen, Afghans have a relaxed attitude to time. Allow plenty of time when visiting someone at home, so that you are not rushed in giving your greetings, having tea, and exchanging pleasantries. Relationship building and trust are crucial in dealing with Afghans, and this may very well take time!

chapter five

PRIVATE & FAMILY LIFE

Apart from religion, the family is the most important aspect of life in Afghanistan. An Afghan holds his family very dear and guards it zealously. To protect his family and its honor he is often ready to give his own life, and even, also, to take a few—an attitude rooted in the age-old tribal traditions of the land.

Even in this twenty-first century, the concept of the large and extended family is still very strong in Afghanistan, something that is fast dissipating in other societies in the region. The large joint family structure dictates how people build their houses and conduct their daily lives. Afghans have experienced more than three decades of conflict since 1979 and migrated in millions as refugees to neighboring countries, as well as to Europe, Australia, and North America. Many have returned home, but their experiences abroad have not changed this family tradition a bit. Even though the urban, educated class of Afghans is exposed to the Western idea of the family unit with its own private space, this is still at its nascent stage in Afghanistan, and one comes across only a handful of such families in Kabul, where adult, working children live independently from their parents.

WHO IS THE FAMILY?

In most parts of the world, a family will consist of immediate relatives related by blood, but that is not the case in Afghanistan. Afghans do not recognize or understand this "narrow" definition of a family.

For an Afghan, distant cousins of his parents and their children are just as important as his own siblings or aunts and uncles, and are treated with equal intimacy and respect. So the entire clan, generally treated as one family, will be included in all family functions and celebrations. When an outsider meeting a family is introduced to "cousins" or "uncles" or "aunts," it is very difficult to figure out how closely they are related, as these terms only have a generic  meaning, and there may be four or five degrees of separation. All these uncles, aunts, and cousins will also take part in most of the important collective family decisions, such as marriage, education, and jobs for children, or in the adjudication of family disputes.

Such close-knit extended family bonds also mean that family members look after each other in times of need. A person in a position of influence or power normally sees it as his duty to support his family by helping them get jobs, or in their business, or even by getting them off the hook if they are in trouble with the law. In the eyes of outsiders, this behavior may be considered nepotism, but in Afghan society it is part of the accepted cultural tradition.

ELDERS AND THE HEAD OF THE FAMILY

Elders have a special place in Afghan society. Elders—both male and female—will automatically command respect and authority from the rest of the family

simply by virtue of their age. Paying heed to their advice or wishes is a given, and it is inconceivable that important family decisions would be made without their consent. Not obeying the decisions of the elders amounts to dishonoring them, and this is something that an Afghan would rarely do. The senior male automatically assumes the role of head of the family, and makes decisions about family affairs. Although in certain circumstances family members might defer to the matriarch—the oldest female in the family—she very rarely has any major decision-making role.

FAMILY DWELLINGS

Everywhere in Afghanistan—cities, towns, or villages—one will come across houses large enough to accommodate a family consisting of parents,

unmarried daughters, and sons with their wives and children. Sometimes the male siblings of the patriarch of the family will live in the same house, with their sons and their families.

The family dwelling is clearly divided into two segments: the inner sanctum, or a space only for women, where no men except close male relatives are allowed; and the outer section, where male guests are invited and entertained. If unrelated

male guests are invited to spend the night with the family, they sleep in the rooms of the outer section. A large dwelling of this kind will normally have a single kitchen managed by the senior women of the family, with support from the younger women and teenage girls.

"The Kitchen Makes a Family"

In Kabul, a few big families now have separate kitchens, but this would be a completely new experience for most Afghans, and is contrary to the accepted definition of a family. "The kitchen makes a family, not living together in the same house," commented an Afghan friend when I told him about some other friends whose brothers, parents, and uncles shared the same house but had separate kitchens for each family unit. [MN]

KEEPING THE HOUSE—DIVIDED RESPONSIBILITIES

As with managing the kitchen, it is the exclusive duty of women to keep the house, while men are expected to earn and provide for the family. The rich may employ some domestic help—a rare exception in a poor country like Afghanistan. In most families, women stay inside the house and carry out the daily housework, and look after the children. Except for a very few people with a more modern outlook and way of life, women do not expect men to share in any chores such as washing, cleaning, or cooking.

Although in most cases women do not earn money, they are expected to manage the household budget. The refugee experience, economic pressure on families following decades of war and unrest, and increasing female education and aspiration have propelled some women into the public sphere to supplement their family income. Also, in rural areas many women take part in farm work. But these working women will always have the double duty of looking after and running the house.

WOMEN, *PURDAH*, AND PRIDE

Purdah, or the Islamic system of the veil for women, is an integral aspect of family life in Afghan society. Families will expect women to cover themselves properly in front of men unrelated to them. When going out in public, women are supposed to wear the full veil, or at least some sort of headscarf. There is photographic evidence, from the 1960s and 1970s, of unveiled women out and about in Kabul dressed in full Western clothes like skirts, tight blouses, and high heels, but no woman would dare to do the same these days, following decades of upheaval and the return of more orthodox and conservative attitudes toward women. Quite a few working women can be seen in the main cities, but they will all conform to the Islamic dress code both when they are out on the street and at their places of work.

The *burqa*, or full veil, is often seen by those in the West as a tool to keep women oppressed, yet wearing it gives women the opportunity to step out of the confines of their houses in safety. A woman in full veil will hardly ever be noticed by men on the street, ensuring anonymity and giving her some sort of protection. Many fully veiled women are seen on the streets escorting their children to school, doing shopping, and running other day-to-day errands outside the home.

There are class, ethnic, and regional variations in the observance of the strict Islamic veil system. In many educated middle-class or rich families in big cities, especially in Kabul, Mazar-e-Sharif, and Herat, many women, young and old, can be seen in public without the full veil, but wearing a loose headscarf and a stole wrapped around their torsos. The full veil custom is followed more rigidly among Pashtun families in the southern and the eastern parts of the country, rather than in the north and the west, where the majority are Tajik, Uzbek, or Hazara. Generally the status of women in these communities is slightly better as they have more education and a little more freedom than the Pashtun women.

Homosexuality

The segregation of women and the strong emphasis on masculinity and male pride can have unintended consequences. Despite its formal prohibition by religious authority, there is widespread acknowledgement that homosexuality exists among various Afghan tribes. Though it is illegal, there is a tradition known as *bache bazi*, or "boy play." There are many historical references to the country's rulers or nobles keeping younger male sexual partners. Even during Taliban rule, the practice continued, and the subject has been dealt with in many stories and novels. There are plenty of lewd jokes in circulation about homosexuality among men from certain parts of the country. Lesbianism, on the other hand, is hardly ever talked or written about, so it is difficult to know if it exists or how prevalent it is.

PRIVATE SPACE AND RED LINES

In a large and extended family, where the elders are expected to make all the critical life decisions, there is hardly any privacy for an individual. So the idea of one's own private space is alien to most Afghans. Everything happens under the full scrutiny of the family, and sometimes of the entire clan.

This complete control of a person's life by his or her family often leads to conflict if the individual tries to break with tradition by making life decisions that are not acceptable to the elders. One of the most important decisions is, of course, the choice of a life partner. Young men and women are expected to accept their family's judgment in this matter.

If a young person were to choose a partner without the consent and agreement of the family, he or she would be in a great deal of trouble. It is not that the family would merely disown them; in many cases the male members would try to save the family's honor by killing the errant individual. Many Afghan families and clans have a long history of feuds that started generations ago, and eloping with someone of the opposite sex from a rival family or clan often leads to bloody clan clashes and revenge killings.

Another big red line is extramarital relationships. Any kind of sexual relationship outside wedlock is considered a total dishonor to the family, and the family or the clan sometimes makes a collective decision to punish the guilty party by execution. In most cases it is the women who bear the brunt, because of the long-established, traditional, male-dominated, tribal culture of revenge. The country's judicial system, which is based on Islamic Sharia law, is also heavily tilted against women who face such charges. So even if a woman is saved from a revenge or honor killing, the judicial system will in most cases send her to prison, while the man is likely to get off.

CHILDREN

It is no wonder that in a country recovering from decades of conflict the experience of childhood in Afghanistan will be substantially different from that in most other societies. It is not only a different experience but, for girls, also a really difficult one, because of centuries-old traditions and the present insecure environment. In this male-dominated society boys are treasured, as in most countries in the region, and in most families sons will be better looked after and better provided for than daughters, who are generally valued less.

   In much of the poverty-stricken countryside,
the concept of childhood does not exist. Most
children have no option but to help their families
by working on the farm, or otherwise taking on
some sort of job to supplement the family income,
from an early age. In this, the experience of a vast
number of rural Afghan children is not very
different from that of children in other extremely
poor countries of Asia or Africa. The same applies
to children from urban working-class families.
However, the experience of urban middle-class
children is different, as their families have the
means and access to facilities that ensure a slightly
better childhood for them.
   Bringing up children is the exclusive preserve
of the women of the family, but the men will make
life decisions for them—about their education,
what they study, what job they will do, and whom
they will marry. Children are normally expected to
be obedient to all immediate and extended family
members older than themselves.

EDUCATION

Most children, both boys and girls, from urban
middle-class or affluent families attend school. In
rural areas fewer—mostly boys—will go to school,
and most of the small number of school-going girls
drop out after finishing primary education. Very
few girls from rural areas even try for higher
education after graduating from high school.

As most Afghan families have had to rebuild
their lives many times over the past thirty years,
they try to give their children as many sets of skills
as possible so that they can enter the job market in
their teens. Many middle-class children take extra
English or other language classes, or vocational
training such as information technology, while
completing their school studies.

School hours are rather short in most parts of
Afghanistan—about four to five hours a day—
owing to the lack of infrastructure, which forces
two or three schools to be housed in the same
building. Thus schoolchildren have plenty of time

to spend on their own outside school, but the concept of leisure and extracurricular activity for the vast majority of Afghan children is nonexistent. Whatever scope is available is limited to male children from urban rich and middle-class families with some means. These boys can be seen in parks playing football or cricket,

two recreations made popular by the global reach of television; they may also have access to computer games. For working-class boys kite flying is a favorite pastime. In the villages children have no such luxury.

Young girls across all sections of the society are totally deprived of any form of leisure activities. They are supposed to stay at home and help the older women with household chores. If they are lucky, they may be able to play with dolls in a small group inside the house.

CHANGING FAMILIES

The large-scale displacement of the Afghan people is almost unparalleled in recent history. Starting with the Communist takeover in 1978 through a coup d'etat, and followed by direct Soviet intervention in 1979, the country has been through massive upheaval with direct war and continuing insurgencies ever since. Millions of Afghan families have been displaced. Many of them moved as refugees to neighboring countries such as Pakistan, Iran, Uzbekistan, or Tajikistan, and many more moved from one corner of the country to another, seeking safety and some peace.

The experience of such a large body of refugees or internally displaced people has had its impact on family values generally. When many families returned to Afghanistan after the fall of the Taliban government in the winter of 2001, they brought back the experience—both positive and negative—of interacting with other societies with different cultures. Women who had never worn the *burqa* returned from Pakistan or Iran wearing one, while many others came back with education and the experience of working outside the home. Economic pressure on refugees, or even on internally displaced people, forced many women to look for jobs to support their families.

Many refugee families who have returned over the last decade after living in countries with better economic conditions were exposed to modern-day household amenities such as refrigerators, washing machines, electric kettles, television, and videos. These gadgets are now essential parts of daily life for many Afghan families and have made subtle changes in the lives of women, particularly among the urban middle class. For them, the running of day-to-day household chores has become easier, giving them some space and spare time of their own. As these women have no access to activities outside the home, their only pastime is watching television and Indian Bollywood films on video.

chapter six

TIME OUT

The concept of leisure does not come easily to Afghans, who have endured more than twenty years of war, conflict, and repeated displacement, and then in the last decade have been trying to rebuild their lives. There is not a single family in the country that has not been affected by these massive upheavals.

The average observer of world affairs will know that, except for a small group of the elite and the rich, life is harsh, insecure, and full of stiff challenges for Afghans. Everyone struggles to make ends meet, so it is no wonder that there is hardly any spare time or money for going to cinemas, theaters, concerts, or sporting events. The average Afghan family will spend most of its free time relaxing at home, watching television soaps or movies—mostly Indian Bollywood cinema, sometimes dubbed in Pashtu or Dari. Only a tiny minority has access to the limited cultural activities that take place in a few major cities.

NAAN AND KEBAB—EATING OUT

The only activity that many ordinary Afghans participate in is eating out, but again this is

confined to the major cities, where there are restaurants and some spare cash in people's pockets. Many neighborhoods in the cities have traditional restaurants, in which people will dine out once in a while. Very rarely will this be a family affair, as only a handful of the bigger restaurants have secluded family sections where women can sit, escorted by their male relatives.

The menus in these restaurants are almost entirely based on meat, accompanied by hot, oven-fresh *naan* bread and sometimes pilaf with a green salad. The kebabs are grilled on skewers over an open charcoal fire, spreading a mouthwatering aroma to all who pass by. Other meat dishes, mostly lamb and beef with gravy, are also available.

Ordinary Afghans now also have the choice of Western-style fast food. This arrived with the sudden influx of thousands of international workers employed by various organizations, including the UN and embassies, along with foreign troops, following the end of the Taliban rule in 2001. So shops selling pizza or fried chicken, frequented mainly by younger people, are often to be seen in the busy business districts of the main cities.

CHIC DINING FOR FOREIGNERS

The presence of a large body of foreigners in the country has also created multicuisine restaurant opportunities for entrepreneurs catering primarily to the expat communities and also to rich Afghans. There are Thai, French, Italian, Middle-Eastern, Indian, and Iranian restaurants located in the upscale, smart, and relatively secure areas of Kabul. These are unfortunately not common in other cities, except for a few Indian and Iranian restaurants in Mazar-e-Sharif and Herat.

These restaurants, hidden behind high walls in sprawling, bungalow-type buildings with gardens, heavily protected by armed guards, serve high-quality authentic international cuisine, the prices often comparable with those in Western cities. Some of them also have excellent bakery sections, offering French or German bread and delicious European pastries. Sitting under dim lights in the gardens, with soft jazz playing in the background, you can easily forget that you are in Kabul.

Some of these restaurants double up as souvenir shops and boutiques, selling carpets, kilim rugs, silks, Afghan dresses and jewelry, handicrafts, drapery, and cushions. These are very expensive for the locals, but many foreigners buy items from these shops to decorate their houses in the city, or to take with them when they head home.

There are a few high-end restaurants where you can order typical Afghan cuisine that will include varieties of kebab, *kabuli* (rice cooked with cubed meat and generous quantities of raisins and shredded carrot), *qurma*, *aushak* (Afghan raviolis filled with spinach or ground meat, cooked in a white sauce), *mantoo*, roasts, and other meat

delicacies. These
restaurants are slightly
cheaper than the ones
offering international
cuisine. All through
summer into fall, fresh
fruit and fruit juices are
served with the food.
This is an integral part of
Afghan cuisine that is
refreshing and energizing.

CHAI SABZ AND CHAI-KHANAS

Drinking *chai sabz*, or green tea, is the national
passion of the Afghan people, both at home and
outside. Afghans welcome and entertain their
guests with a constant supply of green tea in small
cups. The local *chai-khana*, or tea room, is an
integral part of Afghan tradition. In every city,
town, and village locals will gather to have tea and

engage in *gupp*,
or gossip and
chitchat. Some
food will also be
available, turning
the *chai-khanas*
into all-day
diners. You can
read elaborate
and varied
descriptions of
such *chai-khanas*
in almost all the
travelogues on

Afghanistan written over the last century.

The traditional way of making green tea is
simple—just add hot water to a teapot containing a
few pinches of green tea leaves and spices such as
cardamom or saffron, and keep adding more water
as the tea is poured. As soon your cup is empty, it
will be refilled by your host or by others sitting
with you at the tea session. After a few rounds, the
pot will be cleaned and a fresh brew made. In most
ordinary *chai-khanas* the hot water will come from
a tall, cylindrical water boiler with a tap—a locally
made poor copy of a Russian samovar—in which
water will boil all day long for pots and pots of tea.
To save fuel costs, serving tea from vacuum flasks
has become a common sight in houses and
workplaces these days. Tea bags have also entered
the kitchens and pantries of some homes and
establishments—their presence the result of ready
access through the globalization of commodities

and the presence of foreigners. Aside from green tea, the Afghans also like their *chai sia*, or black tea, in the morning—prepared in exactly the same way.

CULTURAL ACTIVITIES

Historically, Afghan culture was based on folk tradition, as well as being greatly influenced by Persian high culture. In the first half of the twentieth century, while the countryside preserved traditional music, simple dance, and storytelling, life in the main cities offered greater sophistication and variety, including concerts, theaters, and film. In the latter half of the century, educated urban Afghans were exposed to contemporary art and ideas through cultural exchange programs with other countries—but all that ground to a halt with the onset of civil war.

After a "cultural black hole" of nearly twenty years of civil war between the Mujahideen

factions, followed by Taliban rule, cultural activities are slowly limping back in some of the major cities. These are more or less confined to musical soirées, with either Afghan classical or traditional music. There is no identifiable cultural quarter, and the only venues where such events can take place are a few government-run auditoria and the cultural centers of some embassies, with access limited to the upper-middle-class elite of Kabul. The lack of public transport and concern about security mean that there are few events in the evenings, except for private gatherings, to which the privileged come in their own cars.

Contemporary rock music bands from Afghanistan have been making their mark in the last few years, but they perform outside the country more often than within it because of the security situation and the lack of infrastructure. Poetry-reading sessions are also common in select circles.

The Afghan Elvis

Ask any Afghan to name a musical icon, and they are likely to say "Ahmad Zahir." A singer and songwriter, Zahir shaped Afghan pop culture by creating a genre that has led many to hail him as the "Afghan Elvis Presley." Unlike other musicians during his time, Zahir had something unique and unconventional to offer his fans—a new fusion of Western pop with music and poetry from inside Afghanistan. Influenced by Western styles, he mixed guitars and accordion with traditional instruments such as the *tar*, *dhap*, and *rabab*. His voice and new musical style struck a chord with the Afghans. Although a Pashtun, Ahmad Zahir sang, mostly in Dari, of love. His songs have stood the test of time, inspiring today's Afghan youth both inside and outside the country. Some of his most popular songs are "Laily Laily Jaan" ("My Dear Laily"), "Dostet Darum Walla Billah" ("By God, I Love You") and "Degar Ashkam Marez" ("My Tears Are Falling Another Time").

Film remains the most popular form of mass entertainment, but because of the lack of cinemas and the ongoing security concerns people stay at home and watch movies on video or television. Several dozen entertainment channels are constantly pouring television soaps into Afghan homes from around the world, dubbed from various languages into Dari and Pashtu.

The Show Goes On

Incredible as it may seem, the dilapidated 1960s Ariana cinema standing in the corner of the Shar-e-Naw Park in downtown Kabul, the front of which is plastered with a jumble of posters, is still running. The posters suggest that it shows mainly Indian Hindi movies, and I always wondered who its patrons were. "Mostly working-class unemployed youths who have no other form of entertainment," was the answer given to me by a colleague who has lived all his life in Kabul. There are very few such cinemas in Kabul, and none in any other city. [N.A.]

Kabul University has always had a big drama department, but theater as an art form has never been very popular in this society. In the current climate it is even more difficult to put on a play because of the lack of an audience and, indeed, of theaters. Occasionally plays are performed in Kabul with support from the cultural centers of a few foreign embassies.

The attempt at reestablishing visual art is also in its embryonic stage, even though some Afghan artists living in and outside the country have successfully shown their work in Kabul galleries.

The only way of finding out what's on in Kabul—apart from by word of mouth—is by picking up a copy of the free English-language handbook-sized monthly magazine called *Afghan Scene*. No such magazine is available for other cities. *Afghan Scene* is available in all the major hotels and guesthouses, and also at restaurants and supermarket checkout counters.

"DOCUMENTA" IN KABUL
The thirteenth edition of the world-renowned contemporary art exhibition "Documenta," which takes place in Kassel in Germany every five years, focused on Afghanistan in 2012. A parallel exhibition in Kabul displayed work by Afghan and foreign artists that ranged from traditional painting on canvas to video art and avant-garde installations.

SPORTS AND GAMES

Like other activities in Afghanistan, sports and games are a privilege enjoyed by people in the main cities. Afghans have taken up cricket in the last decade, after the return of millions of refugees who learned to play the game in the refugee camps of Peshawar or Quetta in Pakistan. Cricket is flourishing in all parts of Afghanistan, and received a boost when the national team won some minor international championships. Such victories have added to the sense of national pride, attracting more and more young people to play the game. You can see boys and young men playing cricket with the most basic kit in public parks, open fields, and city streets all over the country.

The global reach of sports channels through cable and satellite television has brought international football (soccer) into urban homes, too. As a result you will often see boys playing football in jerseys carrying the names of international superstars like Messi, Ronaldo, or Rooney. The national team regularly takes part in various Asian tournaments, though it has yet to make its mark. In a bid to improve the quality of the game and to look for new talent, the country's football association, supported by the government, recently introduced its own version of a premier league, in which teams from the various regions compete. The tournament has already become popular, and matches in the stadiums of the regional centers attract big crowds, which include women.

Kites and kite-fighting are popular with young Afghan boys, and in the windy fall season the city sky will be dotted with colorful shapes. There are competitions in which boys try to cut the strings of others' kites, and then capture the fallen kites.

Another sport that has caught on like wildfire in the past decade—perhaps because the Afghans' physical build and strength suit them to it—is martial arts. You'll come across numerous billboards and posters for schools of martial arts such as Tae Kwon Do and Judo in cities and towns. One youth who won the first-ever Olympics medal for the country in Tae Kwon Do in Beijing in 2000 kindled interest and encouraged many to take it up. It doesn't need much infrastructure, other than a training hall and teachers, so it is easy to start a school in residential neighborhoods, where children and young people can readily join.

Some Afghans take bodybuilding and weightlifting very seriously. Billboards promoting bodybuilding, often unintentionally funny, depicting the most disproportionate human figures covered with waves of muscles, are a common sight at busy street junctions.

Even though there are severe restrictions on dress codes and concerns about security for girls and young women, some are taking part in all kinds of sports and games. They are playing football or cricket, participating in track and field events, and even representing the nation in international tournaments.

Some traditional men-only, high-adrenalin sports, such as archery or *buzkashi*, are still popular in rural areas, where people gather in great numbers to watch the competitions. *Buzkashi*, in which contesting teams on horseback vie with each other to grab the carcass of a beheaded goat, is very much an Afghan sport, and is centuries old. This sport speaks volumes about the fierce nature of the

Afghans and their culture. Many of the influential politicians have their own *buzkashi* teams, which take part in competitions all through the fall and spring, when the weather is good for outdoor contests.

Rollerskating and skateboarding have caught the imagination of some children in Kabul, and even a few street children regularly skate at an arena built and supported by a nongovernmental organization.

SHOPPING FOR PLEASURE

There are two types of shopping opportunities in the main cities, particularly in Kabul and relatively secure Herat and Mazar-e-Sharif. One is for the locals, who go to the newly constructed shining, glass-walled malls, full of shops selling Western products—branded clothing, electronics, kitchenware, or foodstuffs from Europe and America—and the other is for foreigners, who frequent the highly priced boutiques selling traditional Afghan silk robes and dresses, jewelry, and precious and semi-precious stones, or the carpet and curio shops. You will hardly ever encounter any locals in the latter category, and if you do spot an Afghan customer in one you can safely assume that he or she is an expatriate Afghan visiting Kabul, like you.

There have been many mentions of curio shops in the writings of Western travelers, ever since they started visiting Afghanistan. All such shop owners will try to sell the foreign visitor "antique" Buddha statues, or articles such as old knives, swords, pistols, and muskets, old rugs and carpets, or needlework textile wall hangings or throws called *suzani*. Many of these items will be fake, so you will have to be careful when buying gifts or mementos from the old bazaars of Herat or Chicken Street in downtown Kabul, which is lined with the second category of shops visited primarily by foreigners.

Carpet and rug weaving is the only ancient Afghan art form that has continued uninterrupted over the centuries. Both locals and foreigners buy locally made carpets and rugs to decorate their houses. The designs vary according to region, each carrying the signature and motifs of the tribes making them in different parts of the country. Often the carpets or rugs will not be as fine as the Persian, Kashmiri, or Turkish versions; they will be more rugged and rustic, which gives them a different kind of charm and character. Carpets such as these line most houses in Afghanistan.

The experience of three decades of war has now found expression in carpet and rug making. A new genre known as "war rugs" features scenes of war with modern weaponry—artillery, antiaircraft guns, Kalashnikovs, tanks, or rocket-propelled grenade launchers—rather than traditional motifs.

SAFE SIGHTSEEING

The armed insurgency and security concerns have thwarted any development of the tourism industry, apart from some organized visits by Japanese pilgrims to the Buddhist center of Bamiyan.

Afghanistan's main attraction used to be, and still is, its breathtaking scenic beauty—its snow-capped, high mountain ranges and idyllic, serene, and sparsely populated valleys, which have attracted travelers to this country down the ages. But such travels have always been, and still are, associated with elements of great danger—either the threat of armed bandits, and currently insurgents, or the harsh climate and terrain, with little infrastructure.

As a visiting foreigner you may be working for a diplomatic mission, UN organization, international development body, or foreign company involved in the rebuilding of the country. In that case you are likely to be confined to the capital, Kabul, or, with luck, your work may take you to the relative safety of Mazar-e-Sharif in the north or Herat in the west.

In Kabul, the best-known monument that one can visit safely is Bagh-e-Babur—the garden around the tomb of Emperor Babur, founder of the Mughal Empire of India. As we have seen, Babur conquered Kabul in 1504 before launching his India campaign. Even though he had founded a great empire, his dying wish was to be buried in the city he loved. So his son, the emperor Humayun, at the insistence of Babur's faithful Afghan wife, had his body reinterred in Kabul a few years after his death in India. The garden around the Emperor's tomb was greatly damaged in the civil war between the various

Mujahideen factions between 1992 and 1996, but an international project has restored the garden and mausoleum into a lovely place to visit. In the garden is the Harem Sarai, or the Queens' Palace, built by the nineteenth-century ruler Amir Abdur Rahman, where art exhibitions take place occasionally.

The newly restored National Museum is another place worth visiting. The museum was ransacked and more than two-thirds of its artifacts were looted in the early days of the civil war of 1992, yet it still has tens of thousands of objects dating back five thousand years. Its collection of statues and objects from the Buddhist period remains one of the biggest in the region. Apart from its permanent exhibits, the museum regularly puts on special exhibitions.

In Herat, a foreign visitor can go sightseeing safely as the security situation there is a lot better. The imposing old citadel in the middle of the city has been rebuilt with a permanent museum describing the history of the city and the region. Herat is dotted with many mosques and other monuments covered

in the blue and green tiles of Timurid period, in the late fourteenth and fifteenth centuries. Even though Mazar-e-Sharif is safe to travel to, there is only one important monument to see there—the Blue Mosque, where the Afghans believe that Hazrat Ali, son-in-law of the Prophet Muhammad, was buried.

Afghanistan is sitting on some of the oldest archaeological sites in the world, but there has been very little archaeological activity in recent years, for a combination of reasons. Afghans have always been suspicious of the white "intruders," and since the nineteenth century the country has pursued a policy of not allowing foreign archaeologists to work there. The war and the decades of turmoil in the latter part of the twentieth century have not helped. The valley of Bamiyan, where the world-famous gigantic Buddha statues once stood, is one of the few properly excavated and maintained sites, and is still visited by Buddhist pilgrims. Visitors can travel there only by chartered flight, however, as the journey by road is quite perilous.

chapter **seven**

TRAVEL, HEALTH, & SAFETY

Fascinated by tales of its breathtaking scenery and the exoticism of little-known tribal lives and cultures, travelers have long been attracted by the idea of Afghanistan. However, only a handful have actually visited this rugged land of high mountains, and tourism has never been developed here as an industry. A few adventurous foreigners have hiked up the high mountain passes of the Hindu Kush or other ranges, or crossed the deserts of the south or the west, and have chronicled their experiences in charming travelogues.

Afghanistan's history of political upheaval and bloody conflicts breaking out in cycles every few decades is, of course, a factor. From the middle of the nineteenth century until the present, the European powers (and most recently the United States) have become involved in these conflicts, which often started as internal power struggles. During the reigns of King Zahir Shah and President Daoud Khan, between 1933 and 1978, when the country enjoyed a period of relative calm, a modest number of foreign travelers visited Afghanistan, particularly the young. But with the Communist takeover and the two decades of war from 1979 to 2001, tourism came to a halt. Even in the last ten years, little has improved on that front. As a result the Afghans have developed an antipathy toward, and suspicion of, white Westerners.

Yet, currently there is a phenomenal number of foreigners in Afghanistan—something not seen before in the country's history. These days one can meet people from every continent, owing mainly to the presence of the "international community"— the diplomatic missions, the foreign troops from NATO, the UN and its various bodies, dozens of international development agencies, and a vast number of contractors delivering support services to the foreigners engaged in the "stabilization and nation-building project." These foreigners range from the ambassadors of some of the most influential countries in the world to helicopter pilots from Colombia, domestic workers from the Philippines, Gurkha guards for guesthouses, and construction workers from China, India, and Pakistan. Some Afghan or joint-venture private enterprises are also hiring highly skilled foreign professionals such as doctors, engineers, or senior managers to run their businesses.

WHAT YOU ARE IN FOR

The experiences of foreign visitors will vary, depending on where they are from and what sort of work they are doing. One common experience of all foreigners working for reputable international organizations or diplomatic missions is the security briefing, entailing restrictions on their movements. The country's volatile security situation means the organizations err heavily on the side of caution and instruct their staff not to venture out if there is a red alert after a bomb blast or if there is intelligence of a "possible attack" by insurgents. But those are rare situations, and foreigners can be seen frequenting the upscale international restaurants in the evenings and the "brunch" at the Serena Hotel, the only five-star hotel in Kabul, on weekends. On most days foreigners can go to Chicken Street, which is lined with curio and carpet shops, for some shopping and browsing. Kabul city is generally not antagonistic to foreigners, as their presence has contributed heavily to its economy. There are fewer foreigners in the other main cities and as a result they are likely to attract curious stares—which do not necessarily mean hostility.

Visitors should expect to encounter poverty in Afghanistan, which is one of the poorest countries in the world. Begging in the main cities and around religious shrines is common. A foreigner walking in the busy streets of Kabul is bound to attract a swarm of children, old and disabled men, and even some *burqa*-clad women, all asking for "one dollar." Women or children try to sell a small pack of tissues, or newspapers, magazines (mostly out of date), or confectionery for "a dollar or two." At busy street junctions people will tap on your car window and plead for money for food, and boys will offer to clean car windows. However, you rarely come across homeless people sleeping on the streets, as you do in many other poor countries.

While driving around, your car is likely to be stopped at various checkpoints in the cities. These are manned mostly by young Afghan "police soldiers," barely out of their teens, with no knowledge of English or any other foreign language, toting Kalashnikov assault rifles. They

may ask to see your travel papers, so it is wise to carry your passport and other documents with you. Normally they will talk to your local driver to find out who you are or who you work for. Stop and search operations happen more frequently after sundown, which can make newcomers to the country nervous, but you get used to it with time. You will gradually understand that they are only doing their job, and trying to make the cities safer.

Even though Afghanistan now has its own stable currency—the Afghani (Af)—US dollars are used as the secondary currency all over the country. Most big shops and business establishments accept US dollars for any transaction. In the past few years some of the international and local banks have set up ATM machines that dispense both Afs and dollars, using locally issued ATM cards or international debit and credit cards.

VISAS AND OTHER DOCUMENTS

A visa is required to enter Afghanistan. This cannot be obtained on arrival, so you will need to apply for one from the Afghan Embassy in your home country. As no one travels to Afghanistan for tourism, the embassy will want to know the purpose of your visit and to see supporting documents, such as an invitation from an organization in Afghanistan, or a letter from the employer who is sending you there. In most cases, the embassies will issue a single-entry visa, but if you are a frequent visitor you can request a long-term multiple-entry visa, which is easily granted.

If you are coming to Afghanistan to work you'll need to apply for a work permit. Your organization will have to facilitate this with proper documentation, and you are advised to carry it with you at all times. You will need to carry it if you have to travel out of the country for a short while, too.

ENTRY POINTS AND ARRIVAL

The international airport that most foreigners use is Kabul Khwaja Rawash Airport. In the last few years Kabul's connectivity by air with this region and the rest of the world has improved greatly with the arrival of some well-known airlines such as Gulf and Turkish Airlines. Dubai, Delhi, and Istanbul are now the most-used entry hubs for Kabul. There are international flights from Kandahar and Herat to Iran, too, but they are almost exclusively used by Afghans and Iranians.

On arrival at Kabul airport, one does not need to complete a landing card as is usual in most other countries. The immigration check, which is carried out by officers with functional English, is smooth and efficient.

All foreigners are required to register with the Office of Foreigners Registration, either at its counter at Kabul airport or at its main office in Karte Parwan district, close to the city center. It is better to get the registration done at the airport, as the process there is much simpler and quicker. Remember to carry two passport-sized photos with you, as they will ask for these during the registration process, which will take only a few minutes. After filling in a form with your passport, visa, and local contact details, you will be handed a card with one of your photos attached to it. Keep that card safely, as you will have to hand it back at the airport on your way out.

There are land entry points into Afghanistan from all its neighboring countries. These are mostly used for the transportation of goods, but a few are used by locals going to or from Pakistan, Iran, Uzbekistan, Tajikistan, and Turkmenistan. Technically, foreigners can use some of them, but this is not advisable—it would be hazardous for both logistical and procedural reasons. The inexperienced guards and customs officials on both sides of the border would not understand foreign travel documents and would invariably ask for bribes; and there would be the major problem of transportation to and from the border to the nearest cities.

PRIMARY LAND BORDER-CROSSING POINTS

Border Point	Route
Torkham	Jalalabad to Peshawar (Pakistan)
Spin Boldak	Kandahar to Quetta (Pakistan)
Islam Qala	Herat to Mashad (Iran)
Hairatan	Mazar-e-Sharif to Hermez (Uzbekistan)
Shir Khan Bandar	Kunduz to Dushanbe (Tajikistan)
Ishkashim	Faizabad to Khorog (Tajikistan)
Torghundi	Herat to Sherkhetabad (Turkmenistan)

TRAVEL WITHIN AFGHANISTAN

For foreigners, flying is the only safe way to travel
to other parts of the country from Kabul. Apart
from the state-run Ariana Airlines, a few private
airlines have been operating successfully over the
past five years. In addition to domestic flights, a
couple of them, Kam and Safi, also fly to
international destinations such as Dubai and Delhi.

There are several bus services connecting the main cities with Kabul, but only local people use them; foreigners almost never do. For the rest of the country, locals depend heavily on the unregulated system of shared taxi services, which operate under the protection of local armed gangs or strongmen (warlords). Clearly, this form of transportation is not safe for foreigners.

In Kabul city there are a few reliable taxi services that are used by foreigners. Their drivers have functional English and are able to communicate with their passengers. Most hotels, guesthouses, and restaurants will have their phone numbers.

Tips are not expected, but will, of course, be happily accepted. Licensed local taxi services operate in other major cities, but as the drivers don't speak any foreign languages it is difficult for foreigners to use them. They do not have meters—fares are preset according to the distance to be traveled.

WOMEN VISITORS

Afghans show great respect to women who are visiting their country, and feel protective toward them. At the same time they expect foreign women to respect the local convention by not wearing tight or revealing dresses, and by covering their head and hair in public. Foreign women in Kabul do not go around ignoring the dress code. Not only do they cover their body and head while on the streets, they even wear their headscarves in the car while traveling. So it is important to wear modest, loose clothing that will hide your shape, and to have a scarf or shawl with you all the time, so that you can cover your head when you are out in public or going to a meeting with Afghans.

Female visitors will feel most comfortable in the capital city of Kabul, as people there are now used to foreigners. The experience will be different in other parts of the country, where you will invariably attract more attention.

Cover Up
One ex-colleague and friend, working in Kabul, had to go to the eastern city of Jalalabad for work. Although she was from Central America and unused to such dress restrictions, she wore a *burqa* when going out on the streets. She reports that it was a strange experience, but that she enjoyed the anonymity that the *burqa* gave her. [NA]

HEALTH

A number of factors should be taken into consideration before making a trip to Afghanistan. The first thing to be aware of is that it would not be a pleasant experience to fall ill there, as there is no reliable and professional medical system in place. The visitor should be particularly careful about waterborne diseases and diseases carried by insects, as the sanitation system in the cities is greatly in need of improvement. Have all the precautionary vaccinations at your local clinic or hospital before leaving your country, and of course carry an emergency medical pack with basic essentials.

Be very careful about drinking water, as normal tap water is not safe. Many foreigners fall ill after drinking water offered to them while they are out and about, so it is a good idea to carry a bottle of water with you, unless you are going to a good restaurant or hotel. In most meetings and business establishments you will be offered bottled water. If you are offered a glass of water and you are not sure about its quality, it would be wise to refuse it politely by saying that you are not thirsty. Also make sure that you are carrying oral rehydration solution packs, in case of an episode of acute diarrhea, which you are likely to get at least once if you are spending time in Afghanistan.

Avoid eating green salad and raw vegetables. Uncooked food is often not properly handled or cleaned, and is therefore another common source of intestinal infection.

Because of the presence of a large number of foreign troops, there are a few military hospitals operating in Kabul, but it is not easy to gain access to them unless you are part of their civilian wing. There are many government and privately run clinics and hospitals, but even the locals are skeptical about the quality of their treatment or their medicines. So for sophisticated and reliable treatment it is quite common for Afghans to travel to India, if they can afford the airfare and other expenses, or to Pakistan, if they cannot.

This situation has presented business opportunities for major hospitals from the Subcontinent to open up branches in Kabul and the other main cities. They offer diagnostic support as well as some initial treatment plans, and facilitate visits to hospitals in India or Pakistan. Dozens of patients waiting to travel to Delhi on all four daily flights are a common sight at Kabul airport. Poorer patients from the east or south of the country travel by road to Peshawar in search of better treatment, while those from the Herat area make trips to Iran either by plane or by road to Mashad.

The visitor should also be aware of the extremes of climate in Afghanistan. The winter is generally harsh, and it snows a lot. Most houses have poor insulation or heating arrangements, so bring plenty of warm clothing, woolen socks, and hats with earmuffs to protect yourself from the bitter cold. The summer in most parts of the country is blazing hot, except on the higher ridges of the Pamirs, Hindu Kush, Koh-e-Baba, or Safed Koh ranges. Temperatures can soar to 120°F (48.9°C) in the semi-desert parts of the south and west. Come prepared with light cotton clothing and a shady hat if you are planning to go to those areas in summer.

Another crucial factor to bear in mind is the altitude of the country. Even though Kabul city and its northern Shomali valley look flat, it is 6,000 feet (1,829 m) above sea level, and other places you visit may be even higher. You may experience breathlessness when walking briskly or trying to exercise, so come equipped with sprays or inhalers if you have any kind of breathing problem.

SAFETY

You should take safety very seriously in Afghanistan. Attacks happen here—sometimes bomb blasts, sometimes concerted attacks by groups of well-armed gunmen. Foreigners, especially those working for foreign armies or diplomatic missions, have been targeted by armed insurgents, but anyone can, of course, be caught up in such an incident. Most spectacular attacks happen around the heavily fortified diplomatic enclaves or close to foreign

military bases. So take care when traveling through these areas, and keep a safe distance if a convoy of foreign troops appears on the road.

Aside from attacks by insurgents, there have been some anti-Western mob activities when locals felt their religious beliefs had been insulted in a Western country. So it is always a good idea to avoid any large crowd on the street unless you are in the company of your own local contacts and friends.

There are regular safety advisory notices and staff briefings by all the embassies, the UN, and nongovernmental organizations. If you don't belong to any of these, ask your contacts and friends in those organizations for the latest information.

Do not, under any circumstances, get into local taxis or cars that are not known to you. There are many criminal gangs that sometimes rob or even kidnap for ransom. Also avoid traveling alone or in the company of unknown people. It is likely that most of the drivers of local taxis or your unknown fellow passengers are perfectly honorable and friendly, but you should not take any chances.

chapter eight

BUSINESS BRIEFING

Historically, Afghans have been exceptionally enterprising and have demonstrated acute business acumen. They seek out and exploit business opportunities by whatever means are at hand, and know how to impress and charm potential clients. They never put pressure on their clients, and are ready to spend however long it takes to build a good working relationship. Then they use that relationship to their advantage. They are also very flexible and pragmatic when it comes to doing business and making a profit. Thus, building good relationships is absolutely at the core of Afghan business culture.

The ongoing nation-building project, funded mostly by Western countries since 2002, presents Afghans with massive business opportunities such as they have never before experienced. The two decades prior to that was a time of economic decline, but with tens of billions of donor money coming in for infrastructure and capacity building, the world has converged on Afghanistan. This includes the most expensive Western security firms, global telecom companies, health and pharmaceutical companies, and other service providers.

In the first few years after the fall of the Taliban regime in 2001, it was relatively easy to start a business in Afghanistan, as there were few restrictions. With the gradual introduction of rules and regulations governing commerce, Afghans are once again taking a lead in the country's economy. That does not mean, however, that the traditional business culture that hinges on relationships has changed. Nor have they adopted modern business practices such as setting objectives and delivering by a set deadline. Rather they straddle the modern ways of doing things and the age-old tradition ingrained in their social DNA. They will use both models in a pragmatic way to reap the most dividends for themselves.

In the last decade, Afghanistan has received significant foreign investment—a lot of it fueled by the demand for services for the foreign armies, the UN, and other international development agencies. Sizable investment has come in the telecom sector, which now enables more than half of the Afghan

population to own cell phones. Proper scientific explorations have established that Afghanistan is sitting on huge quantities of mineral resources such as oil, gas, copper, gold, cobalt, and lithium. Mapping of these mineral reserves and the subsequent global auctioning have opened up opportunities for an even greater inflow of foreign investment. Chinese firms have already won exploitation rights to the copper, gas, and oil deposits, and Turkish and Indian companies are heavily involved in infrastructure building projects.

As we have seen, there is an acute shortage of power supply in the country, and a very limited power generation capacity. Afghanistan imports electricity from its northern neighbors, Tajikistan, Turkmenistan, and Uzbekistan, which partially lights a few main cities in the north, west, and central areas of the country. The countryside gets practically no power supply from the government.

Most businesses, big or small, make their own
arrangements for electricity by using diesel-
powered generators.

SITTING ON THE CARPET—A MINDSET

The traditional Afghan way of doing business—
sitting on a carpet and reclining on cushions—is
at the heart of the business culture, even in the
twenty-first century. The philosophy behind it is
to relax first and then to get down to business.

Over the centuries there have been many
descriptions by foreign travelers of the Afghan way
of doing business. The most common account goes
like this: if you go into a carpet shop, the owner
will welcome you with cups of green tea, seat you
comfortably on the mattress on the floor, and
exchange pleasantries for at least half an hour before
trying to sell you a carpet or a rug. He will take

immense pleasure in showing you his collection, explaining its origin, the material, and motifs to you. He will not mind spending a couple of hours this way, offering copious cups of green tea, and will not be bothered even if you do not buy anything from him in the end.

While it still happens in a few shops, sitting on the carpet is no longer part of business practice in Afghanistan. Carpets and cushions have been replaced by chairs and tables, and sometimes modern conference rooms, but in the ethos and philosophy of conducting business little has changed. So, if you are in the country for that purpose, bear in mind the Afghans' relaxed business style and be sure to factor in enough time for all your business transactions. You will need to adapt your pace to that of your Afghan counterparts.

MANAGING BUSINESS

As with all other sectors, business is on the path to recovery from almost nothing. The big companies and organizations that normally help a country to prosper were practically obliterated in the past two decades of conflict. The present Afghan government and the Western powers helping it in the process of nation building acknowledge that the economy and business need to grow fast in order to bring stability to the country, but lack of experience and understanding of good governance mean that the rules for

conducting business are still evolving. As a result, many businesses are run in a more informal way.

Hundreds of foreign advisors are working with various government departments to build capacity, but progress is slow. A major problem is the mismatch of cultures between the advisors and the Afghans. The Afghans find it difficult to understand the process- and protocol-driven style of Western business culture—involving, for example, taking minutes of meetings and decisions—as they have, for ages, been conducting business in a different way, which has both advantages and disadvantages. The Afghan approach—which often simply relies on honor and word of mouth without creating reams of paperwork—can cut out massive bureaucracy, making the implementation of decisions easier. The downside of this approach is that there is no paper trail, and it is difficult to resolve disputes.

After-Hours Service

In 2002, soon after the war ended, during a visit to Kabul we urgently needed to get a local cell phone connection for our work. The country's first cell phone network had just been launched by an American-Afghan businessman. By the time we arrived at the company's premises, however, the service area had closed for the day. But by talking to a mid-level manager who was working late, we gained access to the office of the company's chairman, who delivered a phone to us in less than twenty minutes. As we were leaving his office, the chairman said, "You will not get this kind of service in London, Mr. Afroz. You can get your phone today, after office hours, because you're in Afghanistan!" [N.A.]

Afghans are practical and realistic in business. They also know how to wheel and deal, and can drive a hard bargain. Their approach to negotiations will be congenial and will give the impression that they are being accommodating, but at the same time they will try to ensure that they are making the maximum profits from any business deal.

In the last decade many foreign companies have come to Afghanistan in search of business, which is primarily driven by donor funding for the rebuilding of the country. As these companies have no experience of doing business locally, they often go into partnership with Afghan firms. Because the terms of the donor funding also entail proper processes and accountability, these local businesses are now gradually educating themselves in business transparency and protocols.

Some Afghans, who have spent time in the West building up their own businesses, have come back in the last few years to invest in the country. They, understandably, are bringing in more modern management practices. Also, younger Afghans are traveling abroad, mostly on foreign scholarships, to study business administration, and with the spread of the Internet in the cities, bright students are equipping themselves with newer, modern accounting and financial tools through correspondence courses. This generation is slowly changing Afghan business practice by filling middle-management and finance positions in scores of international development agencies and profit-making companies.

MEETINGS

Afghan informality is reflected in the way business meetings are conducted. As we have seen, people have a relaxed attitude toward time and will often show up late, so be prepared for a delayed start if you are attending a meeting where the Afghans are taking the lead. Then there is the common practice of exchanging pleasantries with all the participants. This takes up a lot of time, but it would be considered rude to cut it short in order to start proceedings. Even as an outsider you should ask about the wellbeing of others, which will create a good impression and help you immensely during the course of the meeting.

In most meetings there won't be a written agenda, and discussions will progress organically from one subject to another. You will need to take your own notes, as in many cases you will not receive written minutes after the meeting. It is always a good idea to send your own notes to everyone in attendance, to establish what has been discussed and decided.

Afghan business meetings reflect the broader social hierarchy. Just as happens in society and the family, the elders or seniors will have the biggest say in the meeting, and juniors will generally speak little or simply nod in affirmation. It would be considered impudent for juniors to sound a note of disagreement or dissent with the seniors present. Afghans will be deferential toward you as an outsider sitting on the other side of the negotiating table; but how much importance you will really be accorded will depend on your position in your organization.

The Afghans are hard bargainers when they sense a profit, but they will be prepared to move from their opening position in order to reach an agreement. Adaptability is another of their strengths, which reflects their pragmatic side. This kind of adaptability and pragmatism can also be seen in the field of politics, in which people will often very readily switch sides.

NEGOTIATIONS AND CONTRACTS

The concept of a legally binding written contract, enforcing strict implementation, may be new to Afghans who have not had the experience of dealing with international organizations. For them a verbal agreement constitutes a contract, which will generally be reached with the most senior person on the other side in the negotiations.

Even if there were a written contract, in the event of a dispute a system of arbitration or judicial intervention is practically nonexistent. To settle a dispute arising from a breach of contract it would be futile to resort to the courts, as  litigation is drawn out and ineffective. Almost all business disputes are settled out of court by approaching the "elders" of the organization with which one is in dispute. If this does not work, one approaches other influential persons who can carry out informal arbitration—in the way social disputes are settled by community elders in the form of a *jirga* (council). A middle path is almost always reached in business disputes.

Afghans are now learning to deal with written contracts through their interaction with the donor countries that are a major source of business. Some education and training has been given to Afghans on business ethics, documenting transactions, negotiations, and the implementation of agreements. But the driver in negotiations and the securing of contracts is still personal relationship.

CORRUPTION, FAVORS, AND FACILITATION FEES

Afghans also know how to grease palms in order to secure business or personal benefits—a practice common in many resource- and service-starved societies around the world. To Western eyes this is plain corruption, and it has been a big talking point in the past few years. Some corruption scandals involving high-profile names in politics and business have hit the headlines. This has put the authorities under pressure to deal with corrupt practices in all spheres of public life.

For a more nuanced understanding of what may at first appear to be corruption or nepotism, however, the cultural context should be taken into account. The obligation toward family or clan members is a commonly accepted norm in Afghanistan. People see it as their duty to help their relatives by giving them, or otherwise getting them, a job, business contracts, or other benefits. This has been the social practice from time immemorial, and Afghans see nothing wrong with it. So there is a clear tension between the age-old tradition and the newly imported ideas of the Western donor countries.

The local tradition of giving and accepting gifts can also be perceived by Westerners as bribery and bribe taking. But Afghan custom also dictates

that one offers gifts to others to show friendship.
Afghans do not consider a gift as a bribe, even if
there is a business relationship with the recipient
of the gift.

WOMEN IN BUSINESS

Very few women in Afghanistan manage their
own businesses or occupy top positions in major
companies. Those few who do are in the main cites
of Kabul, Mazar-e-Sharif, and Herat. There is still no
woman in the boardrooms of any of the big Afghan
or joint-venture companies operating in the country.
In Kabul, some women run small boutiques selling
locally produced handicrafts and souvenirs. Most
such businesses have come into being with support
from the development agencies, which are trying to
empower women through business ventures.

chapter **nine**

COMMUNICATION

Generally speaking, Afghans are communicative—
they love to talk. They like to express themselves
in elaborate language, and the country has a great
oral tradition of storytelling. They find immense
pleasure in spending time with friends, and even
with strangers, talking for hours. There are some
great descriptions by travelers to Afghanistan of
conversations such as these in town or village *chai-
khanas*. So if you are traveling in this country do
not be startled if a total stranger comes up to you
and starts a conversation, wanting to know all
about you and your family.

The poor literacy rate also means that people
depend more on oral tradition than a written one,
which is the privilege of a small section of society.
This is the reason radio is still the most popular
form of mass communication, rather than the print
media. Television has taken off, but the lack of
electricity and the high cost of transmission means
its reach is restricted to the main cities and towns.

With the world engaged in the project of nation
building in Afghanistan, the country is making
progress in leaps and bounds in communication
technology, particularly mobile technology, from
a position of almost nothing in 2001.

LANGUAGES

Of the forty-eight languages spoken in Afghanistan, two are the main languages of the country: Pashto and Dari. Pashto is the mother tongue of the largest ethnic group, the Pashtun people. Dari, spoken by the non-Pashtun Afghans, is a variation of Farsi, and is practically the lingua franca. Even Pashtun people will understand Dari, and most will speak it; but non-Pashtun Afghans will not usually speak Pashto. So learning Dari will help you to communicate effectively in Afghanistan.

There is a sizable Uzbek- and Turkmen-speaking population, besides other smaller language groups like the Nuristani, Baloch, and Kuchi.

English

Mainly in the cities and major towns, there are many Afghans who understand English, now more than ever before, as a result of the presence of the Western powers in the country. The middle class now considers knowledge of English to be a "must-have" skill that will ensure them jobs with foreign companies and international development agencies, and as interpreters with foreign troops or in diplomatic missions. We have mentioned the entrepreneurial flair and adaptability of the Afghans. To prove the point, all the major cities and towns saw a mushrooming of English teaching within months of the change of regime in 2001, when the Taliban were defeated by the American-led international force. Afghans who had learned English as refugees in Pakistan, the United States, Britain, Australia, and Iran started opening language schools, seeing it as a business opportunity, soon after returning home.

Other Languages

The refugee experience has introduced other languages into Afghanistan. Urdu has been brought home by the more than three million refugees who had lived in Pakistan for nearly two decades. Many of them went to school there, thus picking up the language well.

Hindi has made inroads in Afghanistan through Bollywood films. A good number of the Afghan elite had always had an interaction with India, where they had traveled for education or holidays. Even today a thousand Afghan students travel to various Indian universities every year on scholarships. Jobs in the Gulf countries have also given Afghans opportunities to interact with Indians, who are present there in large numbers. So someone from the Subcontinent with a reasonable knowledge of Hindi or Urdu can easily manage in Afghanistan's main cities.

During the 1980s, when the Soviet Union intervened in the country by sending in hundreds of thousands of troops, many Afghans learned Russian. Russians set up the Kabul Polytechnic, and Russians came here to teach. They also sent Afghan students to study in the USSR. Many from that generation still speak Russian fluently.

There are sizable expatriate Afghan communities in many countries in Europe, mainly in Germany and France, so you can also expect to hear a smattering of German or French in certain places in Kabul.

BODY LANGUAGE

Afghans have their own signature body language, which starts with their unique way of greeting. Two Afghans meeting will elaborately enquire about each other's wellbeing, even if they are meeting for the first time. To an outsider the earnestness of the conversation will give the impression that they had known each other all their lives. If entering a room full of people, one is expected to do the same with each person present.

While shaking hands, Afghans will use both hands to hold and shake the other person's, as a show of warmth and sincerity. Some place their right hand over their heart with a little bow, a gesture symbolizing respect. It is appropriate and expected that the receiver reciprocates in the same manner. During exchanges of greetings, one is also expected to wear a smile, signifying friendship and amity.

Generally, Afghans are physically expressive and quite tactile. As previously mentioned, you may feel that they encroach on your personal space. In conversation, Afghans will show total engagement with you by making eye contact and showing intent through eagerness. They will expect the same from you. Afghans are quite animated when they talk. They use a lot of gesticulation, facial expressions, and body language, and will not mind if you do the same. But raising your voice is not a good idea, as most Afghans are softly spoken. Speaking in a raised voice will either alienate them or offend them.

There are some universal sexual gestures that are applicable to the Afghans too, but with slight variations. There are some hilarious stories in circulation of how Afghan interpreters have had fun at the expense of Westerners by teaching them gestures that should not be used in public. These have made the foreigners unpopular, or put them on the spot. So be careful about making any gestures that have been passed on to you by local interpreters.

HUMOR

Afghans are humorous people. As a friend put it, "Afghans live on humor as they live on food." Humor is the only way in which they can make life bearable in the face of daily struggle. So they will readily make up jokes about subjects ranging from poverty and illiteracy to political dysfunction, and use them repeatedly in daily conversation.

The Afghans do not have any qualms about political correctness and often joke about things that may not seem right to Westerners. They may make fun of people's looks, eating habits, or weight, right in front of them. But they are good sports, and will not mind or take offense if others make fun of them in the same way.

It is no wonder that decades of war and conflict have given rise to black humor in Afghan society, which sometimes has been interpreted as a form of catharsis. There are a lot of dark jokes in circulation.

Shortchanged!
A young man had been brainwashed to be a suicide bomber. His mentors convinced him that, in exchange for his life, he would surely go to Heaven and have a good time in the company of seventy-two virgins. He went on his suicide mission. He was not killed, but was badly injured and taken to the hospital. When he woke up he was in a brightly lit ward, with a nurse dressed in white, standing at his bedside. He asked, "Where are the other seventy-one?"

In recent years, stand-up comedy has been drawing large audiences in Afghanistan as local television channels have pushed the boundaries with political satire.

MEDIA AND COMMUNICATION TECHNOLOGY

The improvement in the field of media and communications technology in the past decade has been one of the success stories of the West's nation building project in Afghanistan. In fact, it not only a success story; it is a remarkable success story.

When the Taliban took over the country in 1996, the media and free speech were among the biggest casualties. The Taliban shut down all radio and television broadcasting except the state-run radio station. There was no other local outlet providing information to the Afghans on any platform. Only international radio stations like the BBC, Voice of America, Radio Liberty, and a few other European stations were broadcasting news on shortwave.

The scene has vastly changed now. There are more than a hundred vibrant radio stations, which are the main source of information for the locals, operating all over Afghanistan. The state-controlled Radio Afghanistan now has the widest reach through its FM stations in all thirty-four provinces, besides its medium-wave transmission. International media organizations such as the BBC, VOA, and Radio Liberty have also established a large network of radio stations covering all the provinces.

Apart from these large media organizations, some local groups have also come up with their own stations, either as a network or as individual stations catering to every segment of society. A lot of them target the youth, while some women-only stations try to address issues of concern to women. Campus stations are also popular among students.

Television has also become hugely popular among city dwellers. At least a dozen TV stations are bringing news, information, debates, and entertainment into the homes of the rich, middle class, and poor alike. Most stations are either in Dari or Pashto. In the north, a couple of TV stations in the Uzbek language are also targeting the Uzbek population there.

THE TV HILL

The revolution in the growth and spread of radio and television can be witnessed at the TV Hill in the middle of Kabul. This is one of the city's high hills, which today houses dozens of radio and TV transmitters that cover the whole of the Kabul Valley and even parts of the Shomali Plains in the north. Only ten years ago, the hill had a couple of towers transmitting the state-run Radio TV Afghanistan's programs. At night the beacons from the transmitter towers give hope to the people, evidence that the country has made tremendous progress in at least one area.

The low literacy rate means that the print media are really restricted to the small elite and the middle class. There are a couple of English dailies, too, but they are there not to make money but to gain some political influence among the international community living in Kabul.

Telephone and Internet

Besides radio, another revolution has happened in Afghanistan—the proliferation of cell phones. Starting with only one phone network in 2002, the country now has six networks offering 3G services. More than eighteen million Afghans (nearly 50 percent of the population) now  have cell phones, enabling them to connect with each other and with the outside world. There has been substantial foreign investment in this sector, with four main operators: AWCC, Roshan, Etisalat, and MTN. The state-run Afghan Telecom has a landline facility in Kabul, but few people use it as it seldom works.

Internet usage is still in a nascent stage, but is picking up slowly. As Afghanistan is landlocked, it cannot connect with the submarine, fiber-optic, global gateway that offers fast Internet connection to most countries. Domestically there is an effort to connect the main cities through fiber optics, but for the Internet Afghanistan depends on satellite connectivity, which makes it quite expensive. So it is mostly used by offices and businesses; home use is largely limited by the high cost.

Another reason for low Internet penetration is, of course, the lack of computer literacy and the high cost of computers. But young, enterprising Afghans are now learning how

to assemble computers from basic parts, thus making it cheaper.

There is a postal system but it is unreliable and untrustworthy. This has given rise to the business of courier services, both international and local.

CONCLUSION

Now that you have reached the end of this book, you might have concluded that travel to Afghanistan would be too difficult a proposition. We have detailed the trauma and the massive challenges that its people have experienced, time and time again, in their recent history, and these are realities that cannot be wished away. With only this in mind, the prospect of traveling in this troubled and insecure country is certainly daunting—but with the right kind of introduction, the right kind of connections, and the right kind of motivation, you can get beneath the skin of Afghanistan and make friends with its people.

Once you have broken the ice, the rewards will be plenty. The genuine friendship and generosity of the Afghan people will be an experience to treasure. On top of this, if you are interested in history, art, and archaeology, you can immerse yourself in all of them. The security situation permitting, you can marvel at the ancient Buddhist sites of Bamiyan or Mes Aynak, the Hellenistic ruins in the north, and the Timurid art and magnificent monuments of Herat.

The great beauty of the land—its majestic mountains and magnificent sunsets, its high narrow passes and green valleys, its winter snows and colorful spring—will leave an indelible impression, and the taste of its delicious fruits—watermelons, melons, grapes, apricots, pomegranates, apples—will linger in your mouth.

Over the last decade many outsiders have spent time in the country, albeit for work and not as tourists. They may have had scary moments, but they will have had good experiences too. Few will be going home without some very fond memories of the country.

So if you are traveling to Afghanistan, it is likely that you'll be going there to work. This book should help you navigate the initial logistical challenges and at the same time introduce you to the culture of the land. We hope it will inspire you to make friends with this extraordinary country and its remarkable

people. Who knows? You too may be bitten by the famous "Afghanistan bug," and will come to cherish this fierce yet honorable, intractable yet warm, loyal, and unstintingly hospitable people.

Further Reading

Ahmad, Aisha, and Roger Boase. *Pashtun Tales: From the Pakistan–Afghan Border*. London: Saqi Books, 2008.

Byron, Robert. *The Road to Oxiana*. London: Penguin, 2007.

Coll, Steve. *Ghost Wars: The Secret History of the CIA, Afghanistan, and Bin Laden, from the Soviet Invasion to September 10, 2001*. New York: Penguin, 2004.

Crile, George. *Charlie Wilson's War: The Extraordinary Story of the Largest Covert Operation in History*. New York: Atlantic Monthly Press, 2003.

Dupree, Nancy. *An Historical Guide to Afghanistan*. Kabul: Afghan Air Authority, Afghan Tourist Organization, 1977.

Elliot, Jason. *An Unexpected Light: Travels in Afghanistan*. London: Picador, 2011.

Hopkirk, Peter. *The Great Game: On Secret Service in High Asia*. London: John Murray, 2006.

Hosseini, Khaled. *The Kite Runner*. London: Bloomsbury Paperbacks, 2011.

Newby, Eric. *A Short Walk in the Hindu Kush*. London: Secker & Warburg, 1958; Harper Collins, 2010.

Rahimi, Atiq. *The Patience Stone*. London: Vintage, 2011.

Steele, Jonathan. *Ghosts of Afghanistan: The Haunted Battleground*. London: Portobello Books, 2011.

Stewart, Rory. *The Place in Between*. London: Picador, 2005.

Thackston, Wheeler M., and Salman Rushdie. *The Baburnama: Memoirs of Babur, Prince and Emperor*. New York: Modern Library, 2002.

culture smart! afghanistan

Index